Sharper than
a Two-Edged Sword

by
Andrew Wommack

Harrison House
Tulsa, OK

15 14 13 12 11   10 9 8 7 6 5 4 3 2

Sharper than a Two-Edged Sword
ISBN: 978-160683-192-2
Copyright © 2010 by Andrew Wommack Ministries, Inc.
850 Elkton Dr.
Colorado Springs, CO 80907

Published by Harrison House Publishers
P.O. Box 35035
Tulsa, Oklahoma 74153
www.harrisonhouse.com

Contents

Introduction

I have been teaching the message of God's unconditional love and grace for over four decades. In that time, I have literally created a library of teaching materials. For many, when they realize how much there is to learn and study, it must seem overwhelming. That's why I have written this book and believe it may become my bestseller.

Sharper than a Two-Edged Sword is a compilation and summary of sixteen of the most important revelations God has given me. Many have even called this the "Cliff Notes" of my messages. Each chapter addresses a specific topic in an abbreviated form, making it much easier to see how these truths are related and dependent upon one another. For example, if you understand the message of grace but have not balanced it with faith, neither of them will effectively work for you. That is why I wrote the book *Living in the Balance of Grace and Faith.* The same is true about many other principles and truths. Any one of them could be misunderstood and possibly taken to an extreme if they are not viewed in the light of the others.

As you read this book, you will get an overview that will help you put each topic in its proper perspective. You can study each chapter topic in depth by reading the full teaching of each topic, which can be found in my books bearing the same names as each chapter title. In addition, I have created an accompanying Study Guide for this book, as I do with all my books. It is designed to be used in conjunction with a short DVD teaching (as seen on TV) on each of the sixteen subjects. You can order the Study Guide and DVD set by going to our website at www.awmi.net, or by calling our Helpline at 719-635-1111.

The Word says, "And ye shall know the truth, and the truth shall make you free" (John 8:32). But it's only the truth you know that sets you free. Each of the sixteen subjects covered in these chapters is foundational to renewing your mind. These insights will help you gain a better understanding of who God is, what He has done for you, and who you are in Christ Jesus. By establishing these truths in your heart, you will create a firm foundation to grow in your relationship with God, and in that relationship, you will find freedom.

My prayer is that the things God has shown me and that I teach here will help you discover that God has given us everything we need that pertains to life and godliness through the knowledge of Christ. Through that knowledge, we are given exceedingly great and precious promises, which make us partakers of God's divine nature (2 Peter 1:3-4). Christ lives in us, and nothing is impossible if we only believe.

Chapter 1

True Christianity

During the war in Vietnam, I met a lot of men who claimed to be atheists. But the philosophies they were so sure of during times of safety quickly evaporated when danger approached. As soon as the bombs started dropping and the bullets were flying, those same people were crying out to God at the top of their lungs. The reason people facing death call on God, instead of just giving up, is that they intuitively know He is real—they also know He can save them. It doesn't matter what intellectual arguments a person gives. At the heart level, everyone knows there is a God.

Of course, some will claim that they are atheist or agnostic and say they don't believe in God, but it's just a mind game. It's a convenient thing for them to say in order to justify the way they live or to get attention, but in their hearts they know better. At some point in their lives, everyone has known that God exists. It is possible to harden your heart so that you are no longer sensitive to the presence of God, but God has revealed himself to everyone who has ever been born (Romans 1:18-20). It's like there is a homing device on the inside of every person that is constantly revealing the reality of God, and drawing them toward relationship with Him.

1

Still, crying out to God in a moment of stress doesn't mean you have a relationship with Him. A true relationship with God is more than just mentally acknowledging that He exists. Jesus said that not all who say unto Him, "Lord, Lord" are going to enter the kingdom of heaven. Many are going to say, "Lord, haven't we cast out demons in your name? Haven't we prophesied in your name and in your name done many mighty works?" But Jesus will say to them, "I never knew you, depart from me" (Matthew 7:21-23). These people claimed to know God, but they didn't have a relationship with Him. Notice that Jesus didn't say He knew them at one time, but they lost relationship with Him or fell away. No, He said, "I *never* knew you." The people crying out to God in that parable were only religious. They didn't have a true relationship with Him.

The scribes and the Pharisees of Jesus' day lived very holy lives. They lived up to a rigorous standard of outward behaviors, but it was just religion. They dressed a certain way. They blew trumpets before them when they gave away their alms. They prayed on the street corner where everyone could see them. They did all of these rituals, but they didn't know the Lord. Jesus called them hypocrites and white washed tombs that looked good from the outside but were full of dead men's bones (Matthew 23:27). Obviously, not every person who acknowledges that God is real has a relationship with Him.

Scripture makes this clear in the book of James, which says, "Thou believest that there is one God; thou doest well: the devils also believe, and tremble" (James 2:19). That is one of the most sarcastic statements in the entire Bible. It says you believe that there's one God, good job, but you haven't done anything that the devil hasn't done. Satan believes in God, yet we know he isn't in right standing with Him. Satan isn't saved; he's going to spend eternity in the lake of fire that was prepared for him and his angels where they will be tormented day and night forever (Matthew 25:41 and Revelation 20:10). The devil believes in God, but his entire life and everything he does is in rebellion against God. So, just believing God exists doesn't put you in right standing.

To be in right relationship with God you have yield to Him. You have to submit yourself to Him in order to receive relationship.

One night, a religious leader named Nicodemus went to see Jesus to ask Him some questions about the things He was teaching. Nicodemus didn't want to speak with Jesus openly during the day because of the criticism he would suffer, but his heart was sincere enough that he sought Jesus out at night. He was in conflict because he saw the anointing of God in the miracles Jesus was doing, but Jesus himself was contrary to everything that the religious system of his day was educating people to believe. After Nicodemus questioned Jesus, He replied,

> *Verily, verily, I say unto thee, Except a man be born again, he cannot see the kingdom of God.*
>
> *John 3:3*

This is an amazing statement, and Nicodemus was overwhelmed. He asked Jesus, "How can a man be born when he is old? can he enter the second time into his mother's womb, and be born?" (John 3:4). Nicodemus was thinking about a physical birth, but Jesus went on to say,

3

Sharper than a Two-Edged Sword

Verily, verily, I say unto thee, Except a man be born of water and of the Spirit, he cannot enter into the kingdom of God.

John 3:5

Some debate the meaning of being "born of water," but I believe it is simply a reference to natural birth. A woman about to give birth is said to have her "water break," meaning that the amniotic fluid that surrounds a baby in the womb has dispersed in preparation for childbirth. This scripture is saying that unless you have a natural birth—when you were born in water—and then the second birth when you are born of the Spirit of God, you cannot enter into the kingdom of God. The second birth is what we call being "born again." So, just as surely as people have to be born physically to exist in this world, you have to be born again of the Spirit to enter into the kingdom of God. In fact, some Bible translations actually render this verse "born from above" or "born of God."

When God created Adam, He made his body and then He breathed into him the breath of life (Genesis 2:7). The same Hebrew word that is translated "breath" is the word that was used for "spirit" all the way through the Old Testament. In other words, when God breathed into man, He literally put His Spirit into him. I'm sure that if we could have looked at Adam's physical body before God blew the breath of life into him, it would have looked just like our physical body looks. But there was no life in it until God put His Spirit in him.

Your spirit is the life-giving part of you. The New Testament confirms this fact when it says that it is the spirit that gives life to the body (James 2:26). Most of society is missing out on what life is all about because they are focused on the wrong thing. They give all of their attention to the body by indulging and attempting to satisfy every appetite and emotion that comes along. The body is not the most important part of life. The spirit is the real, life-giving part of a person—that's the reason someone can have all of the money, fame, and possessions imaginable and still be miserable. It's why people turn to drugs and other addictions. They are trying to find life and happiness in the flesh, not realizing that what they are seeking only comes through the spirit.

When man was created, his spirit was alive because it was born of God, but the spirit of man died when he sinned. The Lord told Adam that in the day he ate the fruit of the tree of the knowledge of good and evil he would surely die (Genesis 2:17). Yet Adam and Eve lived for hundreds of years after they ate of the tree, so it wasn't physical death God was talking about. They died spiritually when they sinned, not physically.

The word "death" has come to mean a variety of things to different people. Some people interpret death to mean that you cease to exist, but in reality you *never* cease to exist. Although the physical body dies and ultimately decays, our spirit and our soul go on to exist eternally somewhere - for those who have been born again, we will be with the Lord. We also have a promise that God will one day resurrect our bodies, and our bodies will be reunited with our spirit and our soul (1 Corinthians 15). The natural mind thinks of death as the end, but the Bible teaches that there is no end.

Scripturally, death means separation. When Adam sinned, he died spiritually. His spirit didn't cease to exist, but it was separated from God. He no longer had the life of God inside of him. Originally, humans were created to be God dependent (Jeremiah 10:23). We were in union with Him. Sin, however, caused a separation, and the spirit that was within us died. After sin entered the world, we were abandoned to our own wisdom. The very nature of man became dominated and controlled by the devil. It became lustful, selfish, and full of hatred and misery. The sin nature present in man means that hurt, pain, and negative influences don't originate from an outside source; they come from the inside.

After Adam and Eve sinned, they began to produce children and they passed on their sin nature to every person who has ever been born of the flesh—which excludes Jesus. Since Jesus was born of a virgin birth (Isaiah 7:14 and Luke 1:26-38), He is excluded from this sin nature. He didn't get His life through man. He received a physical body through a woman, but His life came directly from God. So, with the exception of Jesus, every person who has ever been born on this earth has been born into sin with a nature that is separated from God and corrupted. This explains why Jesus said you must be "born again," because the spirit of every person who has not accepted Jesus as their Lord is still dead.

Man's separation from God isn't about individual actions, or sins; your actions of sin are a result of your sin nature. You don't have to teach a child to do evil; he or she will do it naturally. The sins we commit don't give us a sin nature. It's the other way around: the sin nature we were born with makes us sin. The Apostle Paul wrote,

> *Wherefore, as by one man sin entered into the world, and death by sin; and so death passed upon all men, for that all have sinned.*
>
> *Romans 5:12*

True Christianity

True Christianity is not behavioral modification. It isn't merely learning to control your actions. It isn't possible to behave perfectly, and God doesn't grade on a curve, so you can't just live better than somebody else and earn salvation. You either have to be perfect, or you have to trust a Savior who was perfect for you. There is no other option. Even if you could behave perfectly from this moment on, it wouldn't change the fact that you sinned in the past. Most people think that God has a scale on which He will weigh their good actions against their bad actions, and if the good actions outweigh the bad, then they'll be accepted. That isn't what Scripture teaches. Salvation is not the result of doing the right things or living a good life.

The Bible says that "all have sinned, and come short of the glory of God" (Romans 3:23). God isn't asking us to meet some minimum standard of holiness. He created man to be perfect, and all of us have sinned and fallen short of that standard. Jesus is the perfect representation of the perfect standard of God, and none of us meets that standard. The payment for the sin we've committed is death. Somebody has to pay, and you can't pay for your own sins, so God sent us a Savior.

For the wages of sin is death; but the gift of God is eternal life through Jesus Christ our Lord.

Romans 6:23

This is where true Christianity and religious Christianity, or any other religion for that matter, diverge. The majority of religions teach that there is a supreme being who created all things, and he is an angry god. To appease this angry god and overcome his wrath at you for your sins, you must promise to behave rightly and deny yourself. In a sense, these religions put the burden of salvation on your back; it's all up to you whether or not you can live holy enough to earn salvation.

Every other major religion, and even a large portion of what is called Christianity, is preaching that you have to earn relationship with God by being good. I'm making a distinction here because not everyone who claims to be a Christian is a true Christian. True Christianity teaches that we could never pay the debt we owe for sin, so God himself became a man and paid the debt for us.

Jesus Christ was God in the flesh (1 Timothy 3:16), and He lived a sinless life (1 Peter 2:21-22). He earned relationship with God through His own goodness. Although Jesus had done no wrong, He was killed on the cross and suffered for our sins. He took our punishment. He sacrificed himself for us. God's anger against sin fell upon Jesus, and He forever satisfied the wrath of God against the sin of the human race. Jesus has paid for *all* sin for *all* time, and because of that, you and I can have eternal life. Not by being good, not by earning it ourselves, but by receiving the salvation paid for by Jesus. Scripture says,

> *For God so loved the world, that he gave his only begotten Son, that whosoever believeth in him should not perish, but have everlasting life.*
>
> *John 3:16*

Jesus has already paid for your sins. The extent of your sin or how good you've been are not the issue. There is only one sin that separates you from God, and that is failing to believe in Jesus (John 16:9).

Salvation comes down to one thing: will you accept what Jesus has done for you?

False Christianity and false religions teach that you have to try to maintain your own goodness and somehow earn relationship with God, but it can't be done. Imagine the time when you will stand before God. If He asks, "Why should I accept you into heaven instead of banishing you to an eternity in hell," what are you going to say? I was a good person? I wore a saffron robe? I went to church and paid my tithes? I read the Bible and tried to be as holy as I could? Any of those answers will cause you to be rejected and sent to hell. The only correct answer is, "I put my faith in Jesus." You might have lived a good life, but without Jesus you can't be saved. And who wants to be the best sinner that ever went to hell?

If you try to stand before God in your own goodness, you are going to come up short. All of us have sinned and fall short of the glory of God. The only thing that will make you worthy to enter heaven is that Jesus paid for your sins, and you have claimed Him to be your Lord and Savior. You have to put your faith in the goodness of God through Jesus. Everyone who trusts in Jesus will be made in right standing with God. Anyone attempting to trust in their own goodness will never be able to live up to God's standard of perfection. The only way to have relationship with God is to have it through faith in Jesus.

Relationship with God is something you receive; it isn't something you earn. When you accept Jesus, you get changed on the inside—you are born again from above. Now, true Christianity does preach that you should live a good life, but a good life isn't the root of your relationship with God—it's the *fruit* of relationship with Him. You start living holy as a result of having a relationship with God, not as a means of obtaining it. Those are subtle distinctions, but the difference is profound, and it is what divides true Christianity from every other religion in this world.

Salvation and eternal life are all about Jesus. Some people try to say that Jesus was a great example of love, but that He is only one way to God. Jesus isn't *a way;* He is *the only way* to the Father. The Bible says,

> *Neither is there salvation in any other: for there is none other name under heaven given among men, whereby we must be saved.*
>
> *Acts 4:12*

Jesus said of himself, "I am the way, the truth, and the life: no man cometh unto the Father, but by me" (John 14:6). Jesus proclaimed that He was absolutely the only way, so either He is who He claimed to be, or He was a deceiver and a charlatan. There are no other options. You can't merely look at Jesus as a good man. Either He is God, or He was a liar.

My testimony, and the testimony of countless others, is that Jesus is Lord. He is exactly who He said He was: the Son of God. The miracles He performed, the prophecies He fulfilled, and the testimony of God the Father all prove that Jesus is our Savior. Jesus is real, and He is alive. He changed my life, and He can change yours. You can know Jesus as your personal Savior and be born again today.

The Word says that if you confess with your mouth that Jesus is Lord, and you believe in your heart that God raised Him from the dead, you will be saved (Romans 10:9). Notice that it has to be more than an internal decision. Jesus said that whoever confesses Him before men, He will confess before the Father. But whoever denies Him before men, He will deny before the Father (Matthew 10:32-33). Receiving salvation has to be real enough that you live it and share it with other people.

Choosing to receive Jesus as your Savior and be born again from above is the most important decision you will ever make. Everything that is seen in this world is going to pass away, but those who know Jesus as Lord will never die (John 11:25-26). If you have come to realize what true salvation is and you're ready to receive it, then say this prayer out loud and you will be born again. It's that simple.

Father, I'm sorry for my sins. I believe Jesus died to forgive my sin, and I receive that forgiveness. Jesus, I make You my Lord. I believe that You are alive and that You now live in me. I am saved. I am forgiven. Thank You, Jesus!

If you said that prayer and believed it in your heart, then you are born again! You might look the same on the outside, but you are a whole new person. Your spirit is now alive with the life of God. You have been set free from the powers of darkness, and delivered into the kingdom of God's dear Son.

Being born again is about more than just getting into heaven when you die. Jesus died to give you eternal life, and eternal life is relationship with God—relationship that begins the moment you are born again (John 17:3). Now that you are born again, it is essential that you learn your new identity in Christ so that you can walk in victory and fulfill the plans God has for your life. God desires to pour out His blessings upon you, but you have to know how to cooperate with Him to receive all that He has for you. So, don't stop here; there is a lot more to learn. In the meantime, go tell someone about the decision you have made.

If you have made the decision to receive Jesus, or if you have any questions, we would like to hear from you. Give us a call on our Helpline in Colorado at (719) 635-1111, Monday through Friday from 4:00 a.m. to 9:30 p.m. Mountain Standard Time.

Additional Resources:

1. *The New You* is a two-part audio teaching available to listen to or download for free at http://www.awmi.net/extra/audio/1039

2. *The New You & the Holy Spirit* is a book by Andrew Wommack that covers what happened when you received Jesus as your Savior, and details how the Holy Spirit is the key to living the abundant life that Jesus provided through His death and resurrection. It is available through the online store at http://www.awmi.net/store/usa/books/323

3. "Eternal Life" is an audio teaching available to listen to or download for free at http://www.awmi.net/extra/audio/k60

4. *Effortless Change* is a book by Andrew Wommack which reveals how the power of God's Word effects effortless change. It is available through the online store at http://www.awmi.net/store/usa/books/331

5. *A Sure Foundation* is a summary of the first four teachings Andrew gives at Charis Bible College in Colorado. It is a four-part audio teaching available to listen to or download for free at http://www.awmi.net/extra/audio/1034

Chapter 2

The Holy Spirit

The Holy Spirit is not a ghost, but He frequently goes unnoticed in churches today. All too often, He is left out of church teaching altogether—as if only people who want to become really mature believers need to know Him. We need to recognize that the Holy Spirit is a foundational part of our lives as Christians. Jesus told His disciples not to go anywhere or say anything until the Holy Spirit came (Luke 24:49 and Acts 1:4-5). Think about that. Jesus' death and resurrection was the greatest news the world had ever known, but He told the disciples not to tell anyone until they received the power of the Holy Spirit. The Holy Spirit is the one who empowers us to live the Christian life. We can't live the Christian life without Him, and we shouldn't try to.

Jesus didn't begin His public ministry until He received an anointing from the Holy Spirit, even though Jesus was God from birth. The angels sang "Glory to God in the highest" and they called Jesus "Christ the Lord" (Luke 2:11, 14). Jesus didn't somehow become God through a process of maturation. He was born God. Yet Jesus didn't begin His earthly ministry until He had received the Holy Spirit (Matthew 3:16-17), and the Bible doesn't mention Him performing a single miracle until after that time. If Jesus needed the power of the Holy Spirit before He began to minister, and if He told His disciples not to minister without the power of the Holy Spirit, then how arrogant is it for us to believe that we can accomplish anything in our own power?

We need the power of the Holy Spirit living in us, inspiring us, and anointing the words we speak. Yet multitudes of people today who call themselves Christians have relegated the power of the Holy Spirit to a secondary issue. They have put the Holy Spirit aside and decided that He isn't important. They don't even want to talk about Him. The reason we have so many people sharing words from the Bible but not seeing results, is that they don't have the power of the Holy Spirit inside of them. They haven't received the baptism of the Holy Spirit.

After His resurrection, Jesus commanded His disciples not to depart from Jerusalem until they received the power of the Holy Spirit (Acts 1:4-5). His last instruction to them before He was received up into heaven is recorded in Acts 1:4-5:

> *And, being assembled together with them, commanded them that they should not depart from Jerusalem, but wait for the promise of the Father, which, saith he, ye have heard of me. For John truly baptized with water; but ye shall be baptized with the Holy Ghost not many days hence.*

After Jesus spoke to His disciples about the Holy Spirit, the heavens opened up and received Him out of their sight. Simply realizing that these were Jesus' last words puts tremendous importance on them. We value a person's last words because it is the last opportunity for him or her to say something important.

This is why people pay special attention to the last words of men and women in leadership positions, such as ministers, businessmen, and politicians.

Jesus was about to turn over the future of His kingdom to the disciples. They were going to be responsible for telling the world the Good News and presenting God's plan of salvation. He was about to put everything He had worked and suffered for into their hands. Jesus' last words to them were certainly important. He said,

But ye shall receive power, after that the Holy Ghost is come upon you: and ye shall be witnesses unto me both in Jerusalem, and in all Judaea, and in Samaria, and unto the uttermost part of the earth.

Acts 1:8

The fulfillment of the promise to receive the power of the Holy Spirit came on the day of Pentecost. On that day, "they were all filled with the Holy Ghost, and began to speak with other tongues, as the Spirit gave them utterance"(Acts 2:4). We would call what they were doing speaking, or praying, in tongues. Speaking in tongues has become a divisive issue, and there are a lot of misconceptions. Specifically, some people argue that the baptism of the Holy Spirit with the evidence of speaking in tongues isn't a gift that God gives believers today. They think it was something God only gave to the believers in the early Church. I disagree, and I think that putting Jesus' last words into context will show that speaking in tongues is a gift for us today.

Following His death and resurrection, Jesus appeared to His disciples on several occasions. The first time He appeared to them,

15

one of the disciples, Thomas, was not present. The other disciples told Thomas that Jesus had risen from the dead, but Thomas didn't believe them. He said, "Except I shall see in his hands the print of the nails, and put my finger into the print of the nails, and thrust my hand into his side, I will not believe" (John 20:25).

Eight days later, all of the disciples were gathered together and Thomas was with them. Jesus appeared in the midst of them and said to Thomas, "Reach hither thy finger, and behold my hands; and reach hither thy hand, and thrust it into my side: and be not faithless, but believing" (John 20:27). Upon hearing this, Thomas answered Jesus and said, "My Lord and my God." Jesus then commented that Thomas believed because he saw, but blessed are those who have not seen, yet believe (John 20:28-29).

We know from Scripture that all it takes to be born again is to confess with your mouth that Jesus is Lord and believe in your heart that God raised Him from the dead (Romans 10:9-10). Thomas confessed that Jesus is Lord, and Jesus commented that he believed it, so we can conclude that Thomas must have been born again. Yet Thomas was one of the eleven disciples that Jesus told to wait until the Holy Spirit was given, so being born again and receiving the Holy Spirit can't be the same experience.

I have heard people try to get around these Scriptures by claiming that this was a special circumstance because the Holy Spirit hadn't been given to anyone yet. Now, they contend, every person gets all of the power and presence of the Holy Spirit they can get when they are born again. But the book of Acts is full of examples showing that being born again and the baptism of the Holy Spirit remained separate experiences long after the day of Pentecost.

The Holy Spirit

In one instance, Philip preached in the city of Samaria and the entire city believed in Jesus (Acts 8:4-8). During that time, Philip performed many miracles, and there was great revival in that city. But then it says,

> *Now when the apostles which were at Jerusalem heard that Samaria had received the word of God, they sent unto them Peter and John: Who, when they were come down, prayed for them, that they might receive the Holy Ghost: (For as yet he was fallen upon none of them: only they were baptized in the name of the Lord Jesus.) Then laid they their hands on them, and they received the Holy Ghost.*
>
> *Acts 8:14-17*

This scripture makes it clear that the Samaritans were born again. They were also baptized in water, which Scripture says you only do after being saved (Acts 8:36-37). Philip wouldn't have baptized them unless they had already believed and were converted. Clearly, these people were born again. So, they were already Christians, but they had not yet received the Holy Spirit. The apostles went down to their city and prayed for them to receive the Holy Spirit *after* their initial born again experience.

This same thing is recorded when the Apostle Paul found some people who were already disciples but were not yet filled with the Holy Spirit (Acts 19:1-10). When Paul asked them if they had received the Holy Spirit since they believed they said, "We haven't even heard there is a Holy Spirit." There are people in denominations all across the world today who could say the same thing. Paul prayed for those men and they received the Holy Spirit and spoke in tongues.

17

The baptism of the Holy Spirit is a separate experience from salvation. It is a second encounter with God when you receive power from on high. There are about a dozen instances recorded in the book of Acts where people received the baptism of the Holy Spirit and in every instance, they spoke in tongues. They didn't speak in tongues some of the time or most of the time; they spoke in tongues *every* time.

Speaking in tongues is a valid gift for today, and it accompanies receiving the baptism of the Holy Spirit. If you don't speak in tongues, then either your beliefs are preventing you from doing so, or you haven't received the baptism of the Holy Spirit. I received the Holy Spirit about ten years after I was born again, but it took me another three years to speak in tongues. I wanted to speak in tongues and I prayed for the ability to do so, but I had been taught so much against speaking in tongues that I couldn't do it. I had too much fear and unbelief built up in me. It took a while to get my mind renewed by the Word of God to get rid of the unbelief.

I'm mentioning my personal experience to show that it is possible to be born again and to have had an encounter with the Holy Spirit, yet not speak in tongues. If you have had an encounter with the Holy Spirit but you don't speak in tongues, it's because you've been taught something that is hindering you. The ability to pray in tongues is important in the life of believers, and it is a gift from God we need today.

Another common misconception is that all miracles and gifts of the Holy Spirit, such as speaking in tongues, ceased when the last apostle died. This argument claims that God only used miracles to confirm His Word until the Bible was complete, but now that we have the Bible, we don't need miracles or baptism of the Holy Spirit anymore. This misunderstanding stems from a wrong interpretation of something the Apostle Paul wrote in his first letter to the Corinthians:

> *Charity never faileth: but whether there be prophecies, they shall fail; whether there be tongues, they shall cease; whether there be knowledge, it shall vanish away. For we know in part, and we prophesy in part. But when that which is perfect is come, then that which is in part shall be done away.*
>
> 1 Corinthians 13:8-10

These verses state that there will come a time when prophecies will cease, tongues will cease, and knowledge will vanish away. Certainly, that time will certainly come—but when? Opponents of speaking in tongues believe it has already come. They cite the verse that says "when that which is perfect is come" and believe that the Bible is what is being spoken of. Therefore, they conclude, prophecies and tongues have passed away.

The Bible is perfect, but I don't believe the Apostle Paul is talking about the Bible in this passage of Scripture. The same passage also says that when tongues and prophecies cease, knowledge will vanish away—but knowledge hasn't vanished away. As a matter of fact, there is a prophecy in the Old Testament that says that knowledge will increase in the end times (Daniel 12:4). Today, you can look around and see that there is an exponential increase of knowledge in the world. The cumulative knowledge of mankind regarding the universe, biology, and technology is growing at a tremendous pace, so clearly knowledge hasn't ceased yet.

Not only does this scripture from 1 Corinthians say that knowledge will cease after that "which is perfect" has come, it also says that we will see God face to face:

> *When I was a child, I spake as a child, I understood as a child, I thought as a child: but when I became a man, I put away childish things. For now we see through a glass, darkly; but then face to face: now I know in part; but then shall I know even as also I am known.*
>
> 1 Corinthians 13:11-12

Now we see dimly, as through a dark glass, but then (when that which is perfect has come) we will see clearly, face to face. Obviously, we have not come to see God face to face yet. I'm not saying that God couldn't appear to someone, but this is a blanket statement that applies to everyone seeing Him face to face. It's talking about the second return of the Lord, or our gathering together unto Him. When we see the Lord face to face is when "that which is perfect is come."

The Scripture also says that when "that which is perfect" has come, we shall know even as we are known. God knows us perfectly, but we certainly don't know everything perfectly right now.

The things that these verses state will happen at the same time that prophecies and tongues vanish haven't happened yet. Knowledge hasn't passed away, we haven't seen God face to face, and we don't know everything perfectly the way we will in eternity. You can't just use these verses to say that speaking in tongues has passed away and ignore everything else that is supposed to happen at the same time. It is obvious that the "that which is perfect" which is being spoken of here has not yet come to pass.

I believe the "that which is perfect" being referred to is our glorified body. Praying in tongues helps us only as long as we are in this physical body and have the limitation of a mind that is not completely renewed. Your spirit is praying when you speak in tongues, and the Holy Spirit can pray through you (Romans 8:26). You are speaking mysteries in the spirit and edifying yourself (1 Corinthians 14:2, 4). Speaking in tongues bypasses the unbelief that is in your brain, and allows you to talk directly to God. It is powerful, but it's only for this life.

When we receive our glorified bodies, we won't have the infirmity of not knowing. At that time, we will know all things, even as we are known. We will know how to pray perfectly. We will see God face to face, and we won't need to speak in tongues anymore. But until our glorified bodies come and our minds are completely renewed, we need the gifts of the Holy Spirit. We need the presence and the power of the Holy Spirit in our lives, specifically the power of speaking in tongues.

Anyone who has been born again but doesn't have the power of the Holy Spirit needs to receive it. You can't live the life that God intends for you to live without the baptism of the Holy Spirit and speaking in tongues; this is the power to live the Christian life. There is a lot about praying in tongues that I can't cover in this short synopsis, but I guarantee that the baptism of the Holy Spirit and speaking in tongues will produce a radical change in your relationship with God. The Word of God will come alive, and you will begin to see and understand things you never noticed before. You need this ability.

The good news is that God wants you to have the baptism of the Holy Spirit and to speak in tongues even more than you want it. Jesus said,

> *If a son shall ask bread of any of you that is a father, will he give him a stone? or if he ask a fish, will he for a fish give him a serpent? Or if he shall ask an egg, will he offer him a scorpion? If ye then, being evil, know how to give good gifts unto your children: how much more shall your heavenly Father give the Holy Spirit to them that ask him?*
>
> *Luke 11:11–13*

Some people teach that you can't have any sin in your life or God won't fill you with the Holy Spirit. They think that God won't fill a dirty vessel. I want you to know that God doesn't have any other kind of vessel to fill! If we could be perfect without the Holy Spirit, we wouldn't need Him. The very fact that you aren't perfect makes you a candidate to be filled with the Holy Spirit. It is God's will for every born-again believer to be filled with the Holy Spirit and to speak in tongues. He created you to fill with His Spirit, so there is no way He isn't going to do it when you ask. The only requirement for receiving the Holy Spirit is to be born again. Jesus is the one who baptizes us in the Holy Spirit, so if you haven't received the Giver, you can't receive the Gift.

One of the things that kept me from speaking in tongues right away when I was baptized in the Holy Spirit was that I didn't understand that I had to do the speaking. The Holy Spirit inspires you, but *you* have to do the talking:

The Holy Spirit

And they were all filled with the Holy Ghost, and began to speak with other tongues, as the Spirit gave them utterance.

Acts 2:4

Just as God doesn't make people receive salvation, He isn't going to *make* you speak in tongues. God doesn't take over people's bodies, so you're going to have to initiate the use of your voice to start and stop speaking. You can't just open your mouth and wait for sound to come out.

As you begin to utter the words the Holy Spirit is inspiring you to speak, the words will come more and more easily. You won't understand what you are saying because the natural mind can't understand the things of the spirit (1 Corinthians 2:14), but you can pray for an interpretation (1 Corinthians 14:13). Receiving an interpretation doesn't mean that you'll get a word-for-word translation of everything you have said in tongues. It could mean that you'll pray in tongues today, and sometime in the near future God will give you a word of knowledge or wisdom. The only time that an interpretation is required immediately is when someone speaks in tongues during a church service. It isn't necessary when you are praying in tongues privately.

Speaking in tongues builds up your faith and draws out the power and knowledge that is in your spirit. If you recognize that you need this gift and you have already been born again, all you have to do is ask God and He will give it to you:

Father, I thank You that I am the temple of the Holy Spirit. Holy Spirit, I welcome You to fill me right now. Thank You for filling me with Your presence.

Sometimes people feel something when they are filled with the Holy Spirit, sometimes not. When I received the Holy Spirit, I didn't feel a thing, but I got Him. Regardless of whether you felt anything or not, begin to speak in tongues by faith. Open your mouth and utter the words that the Holy Spirit is inspiring within you.

Make praying in tongues a regular practice and you will begin to see the supernatural power of God manifesting in your life!

Additional Resources:

1. *The Holy Spirit* is a two-part audio teaching available to listen to or download for free at http://www.awmi.net/extra/audio/1040

2. *The New You & the Holy Spirit* is a book by Andrew Wommack that covers what happened when you received Jesus as your Savior, and how the Holy Spirit is the key to living the abundant life that Jesus provided through His death and resurrection. It is available through the online store at http://www.awmi.net/store/usa/books/323

3. *The Positive Ministry of the Holy Spirit* is a four-part audio teaching available to listen to or download for free at http://www.awmi.net/extra/audio/1020

4. *How to Hear God's Voice* is a three-part audio teaching. Hearing the voice of the Lord is probably the single most important element in having a victorious Christian life after being born-again. This series is available to listen to or download for free at http://www.awmi.net/extra/audio/1030

How to Flow in the Gifts of the Holy Spirit is a three-part audio teaching available to listen to or download for free at http://www.awmi.net/extra/audio/1031

Chapter 3

Spirit, Soul & Body

I was born again when I was eight years old. The very next day when I went to school, my friends could see a difference in me. It was a genuine conversion, and it changed me. But over time, like many Christians, I became stuck in religion. I fell into the trap of thinking I had to do something to earn God's favor. This put me on the treadmill of trying to be good enough to please God but always falling short. Ten years after I was born again, I finally came to the end of myself and experienced a dramatic encounter with the Lord.

On March 23, 1968, I was at a prayer meeting on a Saturday night with some friends, when all of a sudden God pulled back a curtain and I saw what a hypocrite I was. I saw that all of the religious things I had been doing, I had been doing for myself— trying to earn the approval of others and of God. I turned myself inside out in front of my best friends that night, and I confessed every sin that I could think of. At the time, I thought God was seeing the true condition of my heart for the first time—just like I was. The things I was seeing were so ugly that I thought God was going to strike me dead, but instead of wrath and rejection, I experienced an outpouring of His love.

It was an experience that radically changed me. For four and half months after that night, I was caught up in the presence of God. It was like I was gone someplace. I had found God's love, and for the first time in my life, I knew it had absolutely nothing to do with me. I understood that it was purely by the grace of God. You would think after such a powerful realization that I could just live happily ever after, but it actually began a conflict in my life.

I had experienced God's love and joy when I was at my very worst, but after four and a half months, the emotional high wore off. I was left trying to reconcile what I felt in my heart with everything I had always believed in my head. I had always been taught that God's love for me was based on how holy I was, yet I had now experienced something totally different. It was a collision between my experience and my mind.

The mind is an influential force in your life. The Word says that as a man thinks in his heart, that's the way he is going to be (Proverbs 23:7). It doesn't matter what encounters you have with the Lord, the way that you think will ultimately be the way your life goes. This is one of the greatest truths in the Bible, and it is important to understand.

I had experienced the love of God, but my thinking wasn't instantly renewed. You can't have someone wave their hand over you and transform your mind. Even though experiences can have an impact on you, they don't necessarily change what you believe. Thought is a systematic process so to change the course of your thoughts, you have to systematically renew your mind. You have to change the way you think. The Bible says,

*And be not conformed to this world: but be ye transformed
by the renewing of your mind, that ye may prove what is
that good, and acceptable, and perfect, will of God.*

Romans 12:2

The word "transformed" here comes from the same Greek word
from which we get the word "metamorphosis," which is the process
whereby a worm spins a cocoon and later emerges as a butterfly.
If you want to transform from something that is earthbound to
something that is beautiful and able to fly, it comes through the
renewing - the transforming - of your mind.

I experienced God's unconditional love and mercy in a powerful
way, but my thinking was in conflict with my experience. I needed
to renew my mind. I am absolutely convinced that if God had not
shown me the truths I am about to share with you, I would have
lost the tremendous impact this experience has had in my life. In
my estimation, this is one of the most foundational truths that you
can learn as a Christian.

*And the very God of peace sanctify you wholly; and I pray
God your whole spirit and soul and body be preserved
blameless unto the coming of our Lord Jesus Christ.*

1 Thessalonians 5:23

I could teach a lot from this verse, but I'm just using it here
as a scriptural example to show that you have a spirit, a soul, and
a body—three parts. Functionally, most people only acknowledge
the body and the soul. The body is obvious. You can see your body,
and all of us are aware of what our bodies look like. We know
whether we are male or female, tall or short. We also know there

is an inner part of us that isn't physical. We know that words don't touch us physically, but they touch our hearts and can cause joy, pain, and other emotions; that's the soul. Every person instinctively understands that they have a body and a soul because they are aware of those two characteristics.

If I ask you whether you are feeling any pain in your body, you don't have to pray about it and get back to me. You know when you are feeling pain. In the same way, if I ask you how you are feeling emotionally you can tell me: happy or sad, depressed or encouraged. You are constantly monitoring your body and your soul, so you intuitively understand those two aspects of your identity. According to Scripture however, you are three parts—not two. You have a body, a soul, and a spirit. But unlike the body and the soul, we can't sense the spirit part of us.

Learning that I had a spirit in addition to my body and soul really impacted me because I now understood that I didn't have to feel something for it to be real in my spirit. The spirit can't be discerned by emotions. Whether I felt it or not, God loved me. The Lord said,

It is the spirit that quickeneth; the flesh profiteth nothing: the words that I speak unto you, they are spirit, and they are life.
John 6:63

Jesus put greater emphasis on the spirit than the flesh, which is a term that refers to the combination of soul and body. The flesh is what you feel, but the spirit is the real life-giving part of you. If you want to see what your body looks like, you can take a glance in the mirror, but you can't stare into a mirror to see your spirit. To see what your spirit is like, you have to look in the Word of God and believe what it says. You can't go by how you feel.

The spirit is the part of you that has been completely changed, and understanding this is the key to a fruitful relationship with God.

Jesus said, "God is a Spirit: and they that worship him must worship him in spirit and in truth" (John 4:24). God isn't looking at you based on your body and your soul. The real you isn't how you look, feel, or perform in this world. God is seeing us in the spirit, but most of us are focused on our body and soul. The Bible says, "Can two walk together, except they be agreed?" (Amos 3:3). We have to come into agreement with God and begin to see ourselves in the spirit.

Therefore if any man be in Christ, he is a new creature: old things are passed away; behold, all things are become new.

2 Corinthians 5:17

After you are born again, you become a completely new creation. Clearly, it isn't your body that changes. If you were a woman before you got saved, you're still going to be a woman afterward. Tall, short, fat, or skinny, the body doesn't change when you are born again. Neither does the soul become completely new. Personality traits can change over time, but they aren't instantly transformed when you are saved. In order for emotional and personality traits to change, you have to renew your mind.

The Scripture doesn't say you will be a new creation someday or that you are in the process of becoming one, it says you *are* a new creation. It also says that *all things* are new, not some things. The total change spoken of here cannot be observed in your body or soul

29

(the mental, emotional part of you). In fact, it can't be outwardly observed at all because the transformation takes place in your spirit, where you can't feel a thing. It is your spirit that becomes a completely brand new work of God when you are born again. Our bodies and our souls are being influenced by our born-again spirit, but they are only in the process of changing. In the spirit, you are a completely brand new creation. You are a new species of being that never existed before.

If you are born again, your spirit is as pure, as righteous, and as holy as it will ever be in eternity. Your spirit is perfect: it contains no sin, no inadequacy, no fear, no depression, and no discouragement. There is nothing negative in your spirit. Your born-again spirit is identical to Jesus! I know some people balk at that, but it's what the Word says:

> *Herein is our love made perfect, that we may have boldness in the day of judgment: because as he is, so are we in this world.*
> *1 John 4:17*

This isn't a promise that we are going to be like Jesus in heaven; it says we are as He is in this world. There is no way to understand that verse if you are thinking only of the body and the soul, because neither of them is identical to Jesus. We have a promise that one day we will have incorruptible bodies and we will know all things, but that isn't true here and now. Your body and soul are in the process of change, but the completion of that process won't take place until we are caught up with the Lord. The only way to understand that you are, right now, just as Jesus is, is to realize that it is your spirit that has become a new creation. Your spirit has already changed, and one-third of your salvation is complete.

When you die and go to be with the Lord, or if the Lord comes back first and we receive glorified bodies, your body is going to be changed. Your mind will be changed. But your spirit is right now identical to the way it will be in eternity. It's identical to Jesus. As Jesus is, that's the way that we are.

Understanding this truth changed my life. Until I understood that my spirit was made new, I looked at faults in my thinking or behavior and couldn't understand how God could love me. I experienced a touch from God and I knew that He loved me, but I was looking at all of my shortcomings. I didn't always act right or say the right thing, and I couldn't comprehend how God Almighty could love me or use me. The problem was that I was looking at the flesh, but God was looking at my spirit (John 4:24). God accepts us based on what He did in our born-again spirits, not based on what we do.

When I began to base my life upon who I am in Christ instead of on my own works, it radically changed my relationship with God. For the first time, I was able to embrace the fact that God loved me. Prior to that time, I had experienced God's love, but I didn't understand it. And if you don't understand something, Satan will come and steal that truth away from you (Matthew 13:19). Getting this revelation of spirit, soul and body showed me how God could love me: He gave me a spirit identical to Jesus. The Apostle Paul wrote,

> *But he that is joined unto the Lord is one spirit.*
> *1 Corinthians 6:17*

The Greek word for "one" in that verse means a singular one, to the exclusion of another. We aren't merely similar. We don't simply have a little bit of God's power and anointing in us. The Word of God says that he who is joined unto the Lord is one. We are identical. In the spirit realm, we are ounce for ounce identical to Jesus.

God isn't dealing with us based upon our sin and failure in the flesh. He is relating to us through our spirits, which are new creations. In the spirit, we are created in righteousness and true holiness (Ephesians 4:24). We don't have to go out and try to earn holiness or beg God to send it down from heaven. Understanding this will change your whole approach to releasing the power God into your life.

The Christian life boils down to this simple truth: in your spirit, you are as saved as you'll ever be. You're as holy and righteous as Jesus is. You have His faith, His power, and His anointing. All you have to do is renew your mind, and the way you do that is by reading the Word of God and believing what it says about you. It's only the truth you know that sets you free (John 8:32), so you have to meditate on the Word until you know your spiritual identity.

The mind is like a valve to the spirit and the life of God that it contains; it has the power to release or to obstruct the power of God in your life. A mind that is focused on what is going on in the body and soul will shut off the power of God. It forms a two-against-one majority with the flesh, so that even though you have the life of God in your spirit, you won't experience it. Getting your mind into agreement with your spirit, on the other hand, opens up the flow of God's power.

We can't afford to shut off God's power in our lives. We have to renew our minds to the truth contained in God's Word and come into agreement with God's view of who we are. Your spirit is already perfect. When your mind aligns with your spirit, you'll begin to see the ability of God that is in your spirit spill over into your body and soul. Your body will get healed, your emotions will be healed, and you'll see the anointing of God pour out into your life.

Additional Resources:
1. *Spirit, Soul & Body* is a four-part audio teaching available to listen to or download for free at http://www.awmi.net/extra/audio/1027
2. *Spirit, Soul & Body* book by Andrew Wommack contains the foundational revelation to everything Andrew teaches. If you have trouble receiving from God, this is a must-read! It is available at http://www.awmi.net/store/usa/books/318
3. "Who You Are in the Spirit" is an audio teaching available to listen to or download for free at http://www.awmi.net/extra/audio/e09

Sharper than a Two-Edged Sword

Chapter 4

You've Already Got It!

Watching a dog run in circles chasing its own tail can be pretty amusing. Round and round the puppy will go, trying to catch something that it already has. Unfortunately, this is also a picture of the average Christian: chasing after something they already have. You might be thinking, *What do I already have?* You have everything. God has already given us everything we need. Whatever you are currently asking God to give you, has already been provided. You don't need to get God to heal, save, deliver, or prosper you, or to give you joy and peace. All of those things have already been supplied

Getting what we need in this life isn't a matter of asking God, and then waiting on Him to give. God has already given. Getting our needs met is a matter of believing that something we can't see or feel is already a reality. As you believe, your faith makes what God has already provided become a physical reality. Comprehending what you have in the spirit will give you a totally different perspective on receiving from God.

The body of believers, as a whole, knows that God has the power to perform miracles. They believe that He *can* do anything, so they don't have a problem believing that God is capable of meeting their needs. The question people have is *will* God do it? They don't understand that God has already provided for their miracle, so they are in the process of trying to motivate God to act on their behalf.

The typical sequence of events in most believers' lives is that they discover a need, and then they go about trying to get God to meet that need. For instance, a doctor tells you that you're sick and you're going to die, so you begin crying out to God—trying to impress upon Him how urgent your situation is, and explaining everything as if it's the first time God has heard about it. "After all," we reason, "God has millions of requests coming across His desk, and I need to get mine to the top. I need to make sure He knows that I can't afford to wait a week on this one." The truth is that God met all of your needs long before you encounter them. Before you were even born, God had already provided everything you will ever need.

A lot of prayer time is wrongly spent trying to force God into doing something. Our thoughts follow this path: *If God doesn't answer my prayers, then I'll get a prayer chain going.* The logic being that God might not answer my prayers, but getting a hundred people together on the same issue will give me extra leverage. Somehow, people believe that if they put enough pressure on God, then He'll give in and grant their request, so they don't want to let up until God comes through.

When the prayers go out and the prayer chains are formed, people don't think of themselves as trying to twist God's arm, but that is exactly what they are doing. They think they have to do something to get God to answer their prayer, but Scripture says that the Lord has provided everything through Jesus. Jesus paid for your sins and reconciled you to God, and everything you will ever need has already been provided through Him. We don't need to motivate God to meet our needs. God met our needs 2,000 years ago when He humbled himself, became a man, and died upon the cross.

Salvation is not a spur-of-the-moment decision that Jesus makes on an individual basis when people pray and ask forgiveness. God doesn't pick and choose who will be saved. The truth is that God has already paid for your sins. He has already provided the forgiveness that you need. Scripture says, "And he is the propitiation for our sins: and not for ours only, but also for the sins of the whole world" (1 John 2:2).

Salvation and forgiveness are available to everyone, but they aren't automatic. You have to *receive* salvation—but instead of begging God for forgiveness, it's more accurate to say that you need to acknowledge that He has already paid for your sins. God has already dealt with every sin you have ever committed or will commit in the future. Forgiveness has already been provided. If you aren't saved, you simply need to humble yourself and quit trying to earn God's forgiveness. To be saved is to humbly receive the gift of salvation that God is offering you. It's completely different from the attitude of trying to earn salvation, or begging God and hoping that He'll give it to you.

The fact that God has already provided for all of our needs is especially clear within the context of healing:

*Who his own self bare our sins in his own body on the tree,
that we, being dead to sins, should live unto righteousness: by
whose stripes ye were healed.*

1 Peter 2:24

In this scripture, the Apostle Peter said that Jesus fulfilled the prophecy of healing written in the book of Isaiah (Isaiah 53:4-5). The Gospel of Matthew also quotes the same verses to show that Jesus provided for the healing of our physical bodies (Matthew 8:17). Notice that the verse says you were healed by His stripes. When was it that Jesus took stripes on His body? It was during His ministry when He was mocked by the soldiers, beaten, and then led away to be crucified. It was 2,000 years ago that Jesus bore stripes, and by His stripes we were healed! Jesus has already provided healing. He isn't up in heaven right now having stripes put on His back.

Countless multitudes are receiving healing today. In our own ministry, our television crew has documented dozens and dozens of healings. All of these people have received their healing recently, but it was 2,000 years ago that the price was paid. Jesus hasn't taken a single stripe on His back since He went to the cross. By His stripes we were healed. It has already been accomplished.

It is far easier to release something you already have than it is to try to obtain something you don't have. It's a step in the right direction to believe that God *can* heal, but there is still an element of doubt in that approach. It's the equivalent of looking at something way off in the future: it might happen, but then again, it might not. When you begin to understand that *you already have healing*, it's a whole different story. The healing might not have manifested in your body yet, but you will know, by faith, that you already have healing in your spirit.

Blessed be the God and Father of our Lord Jesus Christ, who hath blessed us with all spiritual blessings in heavenly places in Christ.

Ephesians 1:3

"Hath" is just an old fashioned way of saying "already." You have *already* been blessed with all spiritual blessings. It's a done deal, and the blessing doesn't stop there. God has placed within every born-again believer the same power that raised Christ from the dead:

And what is the exceeding greatness of his power to us-ward who believe, according to the working of his mighty power, which he wrought in Christ, when he raised him from the dead, and set him at his own right hand in the heavenly places.

Ephesians 1:19-20

God's power, the same power that raised Jesus from the dead, is already on the inside of you. You don't have to pray and ask God to come heal you; you've already got it! You already have prosperity. You already have anointing. You already have wisdom. You already have faith, and on and on it goes.

I know somebody is thinking, *If I've already got it, then where is it?* It's in your spirit. You can't feel by sensation what is in your spirit. By contrast, your body feels everything that is going on: whether you have pain or feel good, your body instantly knows it. In the same way, your soul is constantly monitoring how you feel emotionally: happy, mad, hurt, or sad, you know it. Because people always know what is going on in their body and soul, they assume that if they had the healing power of God in their spirit that they would know it. But you can't feel what you have in your spirit. The only way you can discern what is true in the spirit is through the Word of God.

Jesus said, "The words that I speak unto you, they are spirit, and they are life" (John 6:63). God's Word is like a spiritual mirror (James 1:22-25). If you want to know what you have in your spirit, you have to look into the Word of God to see what it says.

For one thing, the Word says that by Jesus' stripes you *were* healed. It's already been done. The Word also says that you already have the same power that raised Christ from the dead living on the inside of you. It's not out in front of you somewhere waiting to be obtained; you already have it.

You might think that the difference between having and wanting is insignificant, but it isn't. This is a vitally important truth of God that every believer needs to understand, and a brief listen to the prayers being uttered in our churches today reveals that most believers don't get it. God has promised that He will never leave us nor forsake us (Hebrews 13:5), and that wherever two or three people are gathered in His name, He is there among them (Matthew 18:20). Yet many church services begin by begging God, "Come and be with us today...move in our midst...we need to feel Your presence." They're asking for something that the Word of God promises is already a reality.

The majority of Christians aren't walking in the spirit or by what the Word of God says; they are trying to navigate through life by their feelings. They have to feel chills run up and down their spine or see somebody jump a pew, to believe that God is present. When in truth, God is present at every gathering of believers.

We need to stop chasing our tails. Instead of asking God to do something that He has already done, we should start believing what His Word says—regardless of how we feel or whether we can physically sense anything. We simply need to go by what the Word of God says, and praise Him for what He has already done. If you start expressing your faith and praising God instead of begging Him to give you something you already have, you will begin to see positive results in your life. Faith will rise up within you as you thank God for what He has done. The Apostle Paul prayed for Philemon,

> *That the communication of thy faith may become effectual by the acknowledging of every good thing which is in you in Christ Jesus.*
>
> *Philemon 6*

The word "effectual" means it begins to work. Paul is saying that faith works by acknowledging every good thing which is in you in Christ Jesus — not by begging God or getting a prayer chain together. Faith works by simply acknowledging, or getting a revelation of, what is already in you. That is a powerful statement.

Healing isn't the only area where believers struggle to understand what God has provided. I've noticed that people seem to have a particularly hard time believing that they already have God's love. I can't count the number of times people have come to me and asked me to pray that God would pour out His love into their lives. On the surface that sounds like a great request, but it reveals a lack of

41

understanding that God showed His love for us by dying on the cross. The Bible says,

> *But God commendeth his love toward us, in that, while we were yet sinners, Christ died for us.*
>
> Romans 5:8

God's love for us is without question. There is nothing we can do that will make Him love us more than He already does. The problem people have is that they don't necessary *feel* God's love, but we can't go by our feelings. Feelings are tied to our carnal nature, not our spirit. As believers, we need to walk in the spirit, not in the flesh (Galatians 5:25). Instead of praying for a feeling, we need to get into faith and start believing what the Word of God says. For example, begin truly believing that God loves you so much He gave His only begotten Son for you (John 3:16). Jesus bore your sins in His body on the cross, and He says that He will never stop loving you. He will never withdraw from you or forsake you.

> *We love him, because he first loved us.*
>
> 1 John 4:19

It's not that we love God, and *then* He responds to us. God loved us first, and now we respond to Him. You have already received God's love, in the same way that you have already received healing.

God made provision for you when Jesus died and rose again, and when you were born again, His power took up residence in your spirit. Before you ever got sick, God put the same power on the inside of you that raised Christ from the dead. Before you ever had a financial need, God commanded His blessing upon you in your storehouse and in your barn and upon everything you set your hand to (Galatians 3:29 and Deuteronomy 28:8). You are praying from a position of unbelief when you ask God to give you something He has already provided.

When God says it's already done and you're saying, "O God, please do it," that is unbelief. How do you respond to somebody who is asking you to give them something that they already have? Imagine a father who gives his son the keys to his car: the son pockets the keys and immediately asks, "Dad, can I have the keys to your car?" The father would be thinking, *Why is he asking me for something I just gave him?* If it were possible for God to be confused, I believe that He would be confused by our prayers. We're saying, "God, please heal me," and He is saying, "I know I specifically told you in the Bible that 'by Jesus' stripes you were healed.'" We're praying prayers of unbelief because we don't understand what God has already provided.

Everything that God has made available comes through the spirit. Whether or not it comes out of your spirit and into the physical realm where you can sense it, isn't dependent upon God; it's dependent upon whether or not *you believe* that God has already done it.

Now faith is the substance of things hoped for, the evidence of things not seen.

Hebrews 11:1

Faith acts like a bridge that runs from the spirit realm over into the physical realm, allowing what is in the spirit to cross over into manifestation. Or you could say that faith is like a pipe through which all that God has provided in the spirit flows into the physical realm. If you don't have that bridge or conduit of faith, you probably won't see God's power manifest in your life. It isn't that God hasn't given; it's that your lack of faith is shutting off the flow of His power.

Understanding that you already have God's power in your spirit will greatly increase the degree of His provision that you experience in life. God has placed Himself on the inside of you. In your spirit, you already have healing, prosperity, joy, peace, deliverance, love, and anything else you could ever need. Before a need arises, God has anticipated it, and His supply is greater than any need. No problem or obstacle can come your way that God hasn't made provision for. He has given you the power and wisdom to deal with whatever circumstances come along.

This revelation will change the way you look at life. It will give you the confidence to face life with boldness. Once you recognize that you've already got it, and you quit trying to get it, you'll begin to see God's power flow through you. And it won't just bless you, it's going to flow over and bless the lives around you.

Additional Resources:

1. *You've Already Got It!* is a six-part audio teaching available to listen to or download for free at http://www.awmi.net/extra/audio/1033

2. *You've Already Got It!* book by Andrew Wommack teaches you how to experience the victory that is already yours. It is available through bookstores or the online store at http://www.awmi.net/store/usa/books/320

3. *Blessings and Miracles* is a four-part audio teaching. Blessings and miracles are both from God, but which method does He prefer in meeting your needs? When you understand this and put it into practice, you'll find peace, security, and stability in life. This teaching is available to listen to or download for free at http://www.awmi.net/extra/audio/1000

4. *How to Be Happy* is a six-part audio teaching. Why are some people happy and others miserable? In this powerful series, you will learn the secrets of being happy. It is available to listen to or download for free at http://www.awmi.net/extra/audio/1019

Chapter 5

The True Nature of God

As believers, we recognize that eternal life is all about relationship with God. Jesus said, "And this is life eternal, that they might know thee the only true God, and Jesus Christ, whom thou hast sent" (John 17:3). In order to have a strong relationship with God, we need to know who He is. We need to understand His true nature, because it's impossible to be in a relationship with someone you don't know.

We value old friends because we've gotten to know them over time. On the other hand, we all have people in our lives who we've been acquainted with for years who aren't good friends at all, because we know very little about them. The sad truth is that the true nature and character of God have been misrepresented to most of us, and our misconceptions are preventing us from knowing Him as we should.

Somebody gave me a horse a long time ago. When the horse was born, the owners put a halter on her and turned her out into the pasture. She had been roaming wild for three years, and nobody could get anywhere near her. The people who owned the horse were leaving the property and they wanted to give her to me, but

I needed to capture the horse before they left. Otherwise, they were going to have her killed and sent to a glue factory. I paid two cowboys $350 to catch the horse and break her, but they couldn't do it. They tried unsuccessfully for two or three weeks, and finally wound up in the hospital.

I came up with an idea to catch the horse myself, but it didn't turn out exactly as I had planned. My idea was to lure the horse in with food, and then rope her while she was distracted eating. It seemed like a good plan. I buried a post in the ground and tied one end of a rope to it so that the horse wouldn't be able to run away after I captured her. Initially, everything went well, but I wasn't at all prepared for what happened after I got the rope around the horse's neck.

As soon as the rope went around her neck, she went berserk. She ran full speed away from me, until the rope ran out of slack. When the rope went taut it didn't break, and the horse was flipped up in the air before slamming down on her back. It was like a bad scene out of a cartoon, and it nearly killed the horse. She finally got her strength back and stood up, but the entire nature of the horse had changed. She was broken, but she was also petrified of me.

From that day forward, the horse would start shaking the moment she saw me. She now had a totally wrong impression of who I was. I'm sure she thought I was the cruelest person ever born, but I never intended for the horse to hurt itself. It wasn't my will for the horse to take off running and almost break her neck. It was the horse's reaction to what I did that caused the trauma. The horse didn't understand that I was trying to save her life, she had a completely wrong understanding of who I was. Eventually, I had to give her away because she never got over being scared of me.

In a similar way, people have a wrong impression of God and His true nature because of the way they perceive events described in the Old Testament. The Old Testament contains examples of God smiting people with leprosy, sending a death angel into Egypt, flooding the earth, and destroying entire cities. I believe many people think that God is angry and wrathful because they have an incomplete perspective of those events. God did flood the earth and destroy cities, but we have to put those events into the proper frame of reference to understand His true nature.

Raising children is a long-term process. They develop as time passes, and how we relate to them changes as they grow. You don't wait until your child is old enough to understand reasoning before you tell them not to do things. You can't sit down with a one-year-old and say, "Now Johnny, if you take your sister's toy, you are yielding to the devil through selfishness. And if you give place to the devil he is going to hurt you." One-year-olds don't have the ability to comprehend that. Instead, we say, "If you take that toy from your sister again, I'm going to spank you." One-year-olds may not understand complex reasoning, but they understand punishment. But spankings aren't a long-term solution. You don't want your thirty-year-old children basing their behavior on fear that Mom or Dad might spank them. No, spanking is just a temporary measure until the child matures enough to comprehend reason.

I grew up on a busy city street and my mother used to tell me that if I crossed the street without looking both ways, she would whoop me. She enforced it, too. I looked both ways two or three times before crossing the street, not because I was afraid of getting hit by a car, but because I was afraid of being hit by my mother. I'm not afraid of getting a whipping from my mother anymore, but I still look both ways before I cross the street. Now, I realize that the reason I need to look both ways is so that I don't get hit by a car, but before I could understand reasoning, it was the fear of punishment that restrained me. This difference in perspective is a picture of the difference between people under the Old Covenant versus our New Covenant.

> *But the natural man receiveth not the things of the Spirit of God: for they are foolishness unto him: neither can he know them, because they are spiritually discerned.*
> *1 Corinthians 2:14*

Before someone is born again, they are spiritually dead. People alive in Old Testament times were spiritually dead, and could not fully understand spiritual truth. Our ability to comprehend the things of God vastly increases with our new birth. Prior to being born again, we simply couldn't understand spiritual things. Under the Old Covenant, God needed to get people to resist evil and to resist the snares of the devil, but He couldn't do it by explanation because they didn't have the capacity to understand spiritual reality.

For instance, Satan is barely discussed in the Old Testament, with only fifteen Scripture references (twelve of which are in the book of Job). Satan, or demons, are mentioned more than that in single books in the New Testament. The reason there is a greater revelation of Satan in the New Testament is that when people were spiritually dead, it wouldn't have done any good to talk about the devil. They couldn't understand the spiritual reality, and they didn't have authority over the devil. Yet they needed to learn to resist evil, so God dealt with them in a manner similar to the example I used of correcting a child: He threatened punishment, but He did it out of love and concern for their future.

I remember walking down a dirt road in front of my house with my wife, Jamie, and our oldest son, Joshua, when he was very little. We lived way out in the country and the road was never busy, so I let Joshua run out in front of us that day. Suddenly, as we walked, a dust cloud rose up behind a car that was speeding down the road that intersected with ours. Joshua was nearing the intersection and he was too far out in front for me to physically grab him, so I yelled out, "Joshua stop!" He froze dead in his tracks, and the car sped by—barely missing him. Joshua was too little to comprehend reasoning at that age, but I had taught him through discipline to obey my voice. I didn't spank him because I was mad at him; I disciplined him because I loved him, and I was concerned for his future. The correction I had given Joshua had taught him to obey my voice, and it saved his life that day.

Sometimes we have to be hard with our children. In the same way, God was hard with people under the Old Covenant. Jesus came along and showed us the mercy and grace of God that the Old Testament didn't explain, but there is not a conflict between the two. The nature of God has never changed:

Jesus Christ the same yesterday, and today, and forever.
Hebrews 13:8

Prior to the possibility of being born again, people couldn't understand spiritual things. Now we can. Under the Old Covenant, God encouraged the people of Israel to obey Him by disciplining them. God told them, for example, that if they didn't tithe, they were stealing from Him and they would be cursed. However, now that we are born again and have spiritual understanding, God has taught us that the motivation for giving should come from a cheerful heart, we should not give grudgingly (2 Corinthians 9:7). There is a clear difference between those two instructions, not because God has changed—but because we have.

Our spirits have been made alive, God has written His Word upon our hearts, and now we can know Him in spirit and in truth. We have a revelation of God that people in the Old Covenant could not have dreamed of, and because of that God deals with us differently. In our time, God is able to show mercy to people who would have received none in Old Testament days.

A law is given in Leviticus that says that if you catch a man or woman in adultery, both must be stoned to death. Yet Jesus showed mercy to an adulteress (John 8:1-11). In that instance, the Pharisees tried to entrap Jesus by bringing before Him a woman who had just been caught in the act of adultery. Jesus had been preaching that we should show mercy and grace to one another, but the Law demanded that she be killed. The Pharisees believed that they had Jesus cornered: either He would disobey the Law by showing mercy, or discredit Himself among the people by consenting to her death. Also, if Jesus failed to have the woman stoned, then He would be breaking the Law and could be subject to death by stoning himself. The Pharisees were sure they had Him trapped. They dragged the woman before Jesus, threw her to the ground, and asked Him what they should do.

Jesus knelt down and began drawing something in the dirt with His finger. We don't know what He was writing, but I think it was something that the Holy Spirit used to convict the Pharisees of their own sin. I wouldn't be surprised if Jesus was writing down the names of their mistresses, or victims of crimes they had committed. In any case, Jesus continued to write on the ground as He said, "He that is without sin among you, let him first cast a stone at her." One by one, the men walked away until only Jesus was left standing with her. Then Jesus condemned the woman's act of sin, but He extended mercy to the woman.

The Lord has always been merciful by nature. Until the Law was given—about 2,000 years *after* Adam and Eve sinned—God was relating to people by grace. God extended mercy to the first murderer on the face of the earth, Cain (Genesis 4:15), but the first person to be stoned to death for breaking the Law was a man who was out gathering sticks on the Sabbath (Numbers 15:32-36). The Law changed how God responded to sin, but the nature of God didn't change.

The Law was given for two main purposes: to show mankind God's high standard of perfection, and to demonstrate that no man could achieve that standard through his own effort. The Law removed any illusion of self-righteousness and established our need for a Savior. This is important, because the Old Covenant and the New Covenant are not compatible. You can't be saved partially by your good works and then have Jesus make up where you fall short. It's all Jesus or you aren't saved. The Apostle Paul wrote to the Galatians that if anyone was trying to save himself, then Jesus couldn't help him (Galatians 5:2-4). The Law proves to us that our only hope is to be saved by grace through faith in Jesus so, in the end, the Law served a merciful purpose.

Judgment was carried out upon individuals in the Old Testament: the flood, the death angel in Egypt, and the destruction of Sodom and Gomorrah are all examples of this. But God was dealing with those people from an eternal perspective. He wasn't looking at the end of their life on earth as the worst thing that could happen. He was looking ahead to eternal salvation—and not just for those individuals, but for all of mankind.

Before the invention of antibiotics, it wasn't uncommon for doctors to have to amputate an infected limb. Once gangrene set in, it would spread until the patient died of toxicity. To save the patient's life, it was necessary to cut off the infected limb. This is similar to some of the judgment we read about in the Old Testament. Death may have been a judgment upon those individuals, but the judgment was an act of mercy for the rest of the human race, since it paved the way for salvation by grace and opened the door to the possibility of eternal life.

The Lord isn't dealing with us through the Law anymore. We have been saved by grace, and our born-again spirits allow God to deal with us in mercy. *Hallelujah!* We are finally capable of understanding spiritual things. We are able to know and understand the true nature of God: God is love (1 John 4:8), and His mercy toward us endures forever.

The True Nature of God

Additional Resources:
1. *The True Nature of God* is a five-part audio teaching available to listen to or download for free at http://www.awmi.net/extra/audio/1002
2. *The True Nature of God* book by Andrew Wommack traces God's dealings with man all the way from the Garden of Eden to the present and shows one consistent nature of God through it all. This teaching will answer many questions and leave you with a much greater faith in the goodness of God. It is available through bookstores or the online store at http://www.awmi.net/store/usa/books/308
3. *The Good Report: Why Bad Things Happen* is a compilation of articles in booklet form on the topic of why bad things happen. Available through the online store at http://www.awmi.net/store/usa/books/101
4. *The Sovereignty of God* is an audio teaching available to listen to or download for free at http://www.awmi.net/extra/audio/l03

Sharper than a Two-Edged Sword

Chapter 6

The War Is Over

God isn't mad at you. He's not even in a bad mood. What great news! Yet many people cling to the notion that God is angry, thinking that they need to spend their lives trying to appease Him. They turn to scriptures that show the wrath of God and they contend that God is still angry with sinners, but that isn't the case. At the birth of Jesus, a multitude of the heavenly host appeared, and praising God they said,

> *Glory to God in the highest, and on earth peace, good will toward men.*
>
> *Luke 2:14*

We hear that phrase so much at Christmastime that it has lost its meaning. It has become something that people use to describe the "Christmas spirit," and the idea that we should be nice to each other during the holidays (as if it's okay to be rotten to one another for the rest of the year). But this scripture isn't talking about peace *among* men. Jesus expressly said that He did not come to bring peace:

> *Think not that I am come to send peace on earth: I came not to send peace, but a sword. For I am come to set a man at variance*

against his father, and the daughter against her mother, and the
daughter in law against her mother in law. And a man's foes
shall be they of his own household.

Matthew 10:34-36

When the angels said, "Peace, good will toward men," they weren't speaking of peace among men. Jesus prophesied that there would be rejection, and Paul said that all who live godly in Christ Jesus will suffer persecution (2 Timothy 3:12). Jesus didn't come for the specific purpose of bringing division, but as you stand for the truth, those who hate the truth will come against you. Jesus came to bring light to the world. Those who were living in darkness had their evil deeds exposed and fought against the light (John 3:20). When you introduce the true Gospel message, those who receive it will be set free, but those who don't will come under conviction and fight against you.

It was never prophesied that Jesus would bring peace *among* men in our time. There isn't going to be peace on earth until the Prince of Peace comes and establishes His kingdom, physically reigning over this earth. No, Luke 2:14 isn't talking about peace among men; it is talking about peace from God *toward* men.

When man sinned, God declared war on sin. He set Himself against evil and man got caught in the middle of the war. Sometimes in war, collateral damage is inflicted while you are trying to defeat the enemy. Because of the sin nature and the decisions made by man, people were tangled up with evil and were targeted in God's fight against sin. God was right to be upset and angry over the sin of people in the Old Testament, and His punishments were just, but things have changed. God isn't at war with sin anymore. Jesus won the fight.

God's wrath and punishment against sin in the Old Testament isn't seen in the New Testament. For instance, Elijah called down fire from heaven and killed 102 men, but when Jesus' disciples wanted to do the same thing, Jesus rebuked them saying, "Ye know not what manner of spirit ye are of. For the Son of man is not come to destroy men's lives, but to save them" (Luke 9:55-56). In the New Covenant, after Jesus came, the war ended. Jesus forever satisfied God's demand for justice and payment for sin. Jesus bore our sin and suffered for us. He took all of God's anger against sin upon Himself, and now the wrath of God has been totally satisfied. Scripture says,

> *And I, if I be lifted up from the earth, will draw all men unto me.*
>
> *John 12:32*

This verse is commonly interpreted to mean that when the Gospel of Jesus Christ is preached properly, then everyone is going to turn to the Lord. I thought the same thing when I first started in ministry, but it isn't an observable truth.

Preaching the Gospel correctly isn't what draws large numbers of people. Some of the largest churches today aren't necessarily teaching the absolute truth of God's Word. They often water down the Gospel message to fifteen minutes of uplifting self-help, to the point where they aren't even ministering the Word of God. Those types of churches draw large numbers of people by offering entertainment, but they aren't producing true disciples.

I'm not putting mega-churches down, I'm just trying to emphasize that preaching Christ doesn't draw all men. Ministers who are really preaching the Word of God and taking a stand for truth do not always have the biggest churches. You simply won't witness the interpretation of this scripture that says that preaching Jesus Christ draws all men, and I don't think this verse is talking about that. Not everyone believes and is saved when they hear the Good News.

If you look at John 12:32 again, you'll notice that the word "men" is in italics—that means the word is implied, but not present in the original language. The translators added the word "men" because they felt it was necessary to clarify the meaning of the original Greek sentence. At least the King James Version translators had the integrity to show their additions in italics. I believe it can be shown that "men" is not the subject Jesus was speaking of in this passage.

In context, Jesus was talking about the sins of this world and the judgment for those sins. The preceding verse says, "Now is the judgment of this world: now shall the prince of this world be cast out" (John 12:31). So, in the next verse if we are going to insert a subject to clarify the meaning, drawing from the preceding thought, it should be the word "judgment." The passage would then read, "And I, if I be lifted up from the earth, will draw all *judgment* to me."

Jesus didn't mean that we would glorify Him by preaching the Gospel when He said, "If I be lifted up." He was talking about being lifted up on the cross. He was speaking of His crucifixion—when He drew all judgment to Himself. The next verse clarifies that, "This he said, signifying what death he should die" (John 12:33).

All of God's wrath came upon Jesus, not just a portion of it. Jesus was like a lightning rod: when He was lifted up on the cross, all of the anger and punishment of God toward the sin of men came upon the physical body of Jesus. God satisfied every demand of justice by punishing His own Son for our sins, and not only for the sin committed up until that time, but for all sin for all time (Hebrews 9:28). Every single sin—past, present, and future—was satisfied (Hebrews 9:12; 10:10, 14). Jesus suffered the wrath and rejection of God that we might be made the righteousness of God in Him. As a result, God isn't mad anymore. Jesus bore our punishment, and the war is over.

The angels were proclaiming a prophecy when they said, "on earth peace, good will toward men." Jesus hadn't paid the price yet, but His birth was a significant indication that the time had come. Salvation was imminent. Another prophecy about Jesus spoken through Isaiah the prophet said,

> *Comfort ye, comfort ye my people, saith your God. Speak ye comfortably to Jerusalem, and cry unto her, that her warfare is accomplished, that her iniquity is pardoned: for she hath received of the LORD'S hand double for all her sins.*
>
> *Isaiah 40:1-2*

The Jews have suffered a lot through history, but no amount of human suffering could pay the price for sin. The New Testament quoted from the context of this passage and applied it to Jesus the Messiah (Matthew 3:3, Mark 1:3, and Luke 3:4-5). This scripture is prophesying about the time when Jesus would suffer on the cross, and draw all judgment to Himself.

Jesus abolished the Law upon the cross and brought peace between God and man (Ephesians 2:15). That is such a tremendous statement that some people just can't believe it is true. They can't believe that one person's suffering could atone for the sins of all of the billions and billions of people who have ever lived—or will ever live—on the face of the earth. The difficulty in comprehending this arises because we don't understand the value God placed upon His Son. Jesus wasn't only a man; He was God in the flesh of a man. His life as God was worth more than the entire human race put together.

Jesus was God manifest in the flesh. Through His suffering and death, He paid more than twice what the entire human race owed for sin (Isaiah 40:1-2). Some churches are preaching that every time you sin, it's a new infraction against God and He won't answer your prayers or fellowship with you until you get right with Him again. They are saying that the war isn't over. They think there is just a temporary lull in the hostilities. The moment you sin, they say, God's wrath is rekindled against you. Essentially, they are saying that Jesus' sacrifice wasn't enough to atone for sin. They are teaching that atonement is in Jesus' suffering *plus* your suffering, but that isn't true. Jesus' suffering alone more than paid the price.

God isn't holding sin against you anymore, but that doesn't mean you can go live in sin. God still loves you if you are living in sin, but sin is dangerous because it opens up a door to the devil (Romans 6:16). The devil only comes to steal, kill, and destroy (John 10:10), so you don't want to open yourself up to his attacks. You're foolish if you live that way, but God still loves you. He isn't mad at you, because His war against sin is over. There is peace from God toward you, and it all centers on Jesus. If you accept Jesus who paid for your sins, then God is not angry at you.

Jesus took our punishment. He suffered for our sins so we don't have to. We can have relationship with God simply by humbling ourselves and receiving our forgiveness as a free gift. This might sound too good to be real, but it's absolutely true. When Jesus was lifted up on the cross, He drew all judgment for sin unto Himself, and now the war is over. God is at peace with you.

Additional Resources:

1. *The War Is Over* is a five-part audio teaching available to listen to or download for free at http://www.awmi.net/extra/audio/1053

2. *The War Is Over* book by Andrew Wommack shows how the longest conflict in history lasted 4000 years and ended in a decisive victory nearly 2000 years ago—in Jesus' death and resurrection. The answers in this book will release you from the condemnation of judgment and fear. It will free you to receive the promised blessings of God! It is available through bookstores or the online store at http://www.awmi.net/store/usa/books/326

3. *How to Deal with Temptation* is a five-part audio teaching that shows us the right way and the wrong way to respond when tempted, and the way to avoid being tempted altogether. It is available to listen to or download for free at http://www.awmi.net/extra/audio/1049

Sharper than a Two-Edged Sword

Chapter 7

Grace, the Power of the Gospel

The good news is that the Gospel will set you free. The bad news is that not everyone is preaching the Gospel. Gospel literally means "good news." It's an obscure Greek word that is used only twice in literature outside of the New Testament scriptures, and it is probably better translated "nearly-too-good-to-be-true news!" We're talking about the kind of news that will make you want to jump up and shout. The Gospel is over-the-top good news. It's the "you just won the lottery!" kind of good news. Outside of what God has done for us, we don't receive news in this world of such magnitude, but the grace of God is that *nearly-too-good-to-be-true* news. It's the unmerited, undeserved favor of God that He lavishes upon us, and when you get a revelation of God's grace, it will set you free. It will make you want to shout about the goodness of God—and hope that everybody is listening:

> *For I am not ashamed of the gospel of Christ: for it is the power of God unto salvation to every one that believeth; to the Jew first, and also to the Greek. For therein is the righteousness of God revealed from faith to faith: as it is written, The just shall live by faith.*
>
> *Romans 1:16-17*

The book of Romans is a description of what God has done for us independent of what we deserve. It's a description of grace, and the Apostle Paul says in these verses that grace is the power that reveals the righteousness of God.

To get the full impact of what Paul is saying, you have to understand the religious mindset of his day. His was a world in which the religious system had degenerated, or devolved, into a list of do's and don'ts. They had laws for everything. It reached such extremes that one group, the Essenes, had a rule against having bowel movements on the Sabbath. They classified it as work, and you couldn't work on the Sabbath. You couldn't even spit in the dirt, because doing so would make mud, and making anything was work. It sounds like a joke, but that was the way they thought.

Jesus' disciples were hungry as they walked through a field of grain on one particular Sabbath day, so they picked grain and ate it (Luke 6:1-6). In order to free the kernel of wheat from the husk that surrounded it, they rubbed the grain in their hands. The Pharisees interpreted what they were doing as work and accused them of breaking the Sabbath laws. It was a false accusation, because there was no direct command in the Old Testament about not rubbing your hands together, but it shows how limiting life had become under the religious mindset of the day.

Religious leaders had been adding their own rules to the Law for centuries. The religious system that Paul was preaching against was all bad news. It was all "you can't do this or that and you'll be cursed if you do the other thing." It was a negative, harsh system with a tremendous amount of wrath. People were being stoned to death for breaking the Law.

Grace, The Power of the Gospel

When Paul said that he wasn't ashamed of the Gospel of Christ, he was simultaneously saying that the religious mindset was nonsense. "Gospel" was a term that wasn't even in use prior to Paul applying it to the grace of God, so people knew he was talking about over-the-top good news. This Gospel was completely opposed to the religious system, which was using fear to drive people to follow God. The Gospel was drawing people to salvation by the love of God.

The word "salvation" doesn't only apply to forgiveness of sins. The Greek word for salvation is *soteria*, and it literally means saved or delivered. It's talking about being set free: spirit, soul, and body. Salvation is not just limited to the forgiveness of your sins. Salvation is also when a person who was sick is healed, or when someone who was depressed receives the joy of the Lord. In fact, the Greek word *sozo* is used interchangeably in the New Testament to mean to save, to make whole, or to heal.

The Gospel of Jesus Christ doesn't only save us from sin; it also saves us from the consequences of sin, such as oppression, depression, sickness, disease, and poverty. So, when this scripture says that the Gospel "is the power of God unto salvation," you could understand it to say that that the Gospel is the power of God for healing, peace of mind, joy, and prosperity. Whatever you need, can be found in the Gospel.

Unfortunately, the Gospel of Christ isn't always presented as *nearly-too-good-to-be-true* news. Some ministers are preaching that God is angry at you and you had better repent, or else. "Repent," they say, "or you're going to burn in hell for all eternity." There is no good news in that—certainly nothing that is *nearly-too-good-to-*

be-true. The turn-or-burn style of preaching is an attempt to drive people to God out of fear, much as the religious system of Jesus' day was doing. It may work, but it isn't the Gospel.

It's true that we have all sinned and come short of the glory of God (Romans 3:23), and anyone who rejects the salvation of Jesus is going to hell (Romans 6:23). So, it's not wrong to tell people that there is a hell and, because of our sins, we're all headed there unless we repent. Those are true statements, but that isn't the Gospel message. There's no good news in threatening people with hell, and fear doesn't set you free to receive the power of the Gospel.

The vast majority of people already know that they are sinners, and most know they are separated from God. There are, however, some who have deceived themselves into thinking that they are right with God when they aren't—people who are trusting in their own goodness. In those cases, it could be necessary to use the Law to show them their need for a savior.

The parable of the Pharisee and the publican is a good example of when to use the Law to point out the need for a savior (Luke 18:9-14). Jesus specifically spoke this parable to those who were trusting in their own righteousness. The story tells of two men who went to the Temple to pray. One was a Pharisee who, in his prayer, thanked God that he was not a depraved sinner like the publican standing next to him. The Pharisee was a man who tithed of all he had and fasted twice a week. The publican, on the other hand, stood far off, afraid to even lift his eyes to heaven, and begged God for mercy. Jesus said it was the publican who went away justified, not the Pharisee. This parable demonstrates that it is the sinner who humbles himself before God who is made righteous, not the proud man living a holy life.

The irony of a strict religious system is that it can lead to pride and arrogance in those who believe they are able to keep the code. They compare themselves to others and think they are doing just fine with God. The truth is, they may be a better sinner than someone else, but they're still a sinner—and who wants to be the best sinner who ever went to hell? In cases like this, it would be appropriate to use the Word of God to point out just how sinful they really are. The Bible says,

We know that the law is good, if a man use it lawfully.
1 Timothy 1:8

But the Law isn't made for a righteous man (1 Timothy 1:9). According to the Word of God, any person who believes in Jesus has been "made the righteousness of God" (2 Corinthians 5:21). So, the Law isn't meant to be used against born-again Christians. The Law is meant for unbelievers who don't understand their need for a savior. It's okay to use the Law for that purpose, but it shouldn't be used to try to prod born-again believers into improving their relationship with God, or to frighten unbelievers into repenting from an angry God. God isn't angry anymore (Luke 2:14). Jesus took all of God's wrath against sin in His own body on the cross (John 12:32 and 1 Peter 2:24).

Paul wasn't ashamed to tell people the Good News. He wasn't ashamed to not beat people over the head with their sinfulness and inadequacy. The vast majority of people don't need to have their sin amplified before them. What they need is to hear the *nearly-too-*

67

good-to-be-true news that Jesus died to make them righteous, and all they need to do is believe.

The man who helped get me really excited about the Lord when I was a teenager had been raised in a religious environment. He knew that God was real, but before he was saved he lived a sinful lifestyle. His problems with alcohol and sexual immorality were well known in the community. A man from my church used to go to this man's house every Saturday to tell him what a sinner he was and how he'd better repent. But my friend already knew he was a sinner. He didn't need to hear more information about how sorry and ungodly he was. He was saved when he learned about the grace of God through the Gospel of Jesus Christ.

A lot of people today are in the same situation that my friend was in. They are being turned off and driven away from God by religion. Religion is pounding them with how sinful and sorry they are, but they already know that at the heart level—even if they won't admit it. What they need is to hear the Gospel, the good news that Jesus died to take their sin and to return them to right relationship with the Father.

We have all sinned and fallen short of the glory of God (Romans 3:23), and the wages of sin is death (Romans 6:23). Even if we could quit sinning from this moment forth, it would do nothing to erase what we have done in the past. There is nothing we can do to save ourselves. In the midst of that hopeless situation, God sent His Son to live a holy life and to earn everything that we could not, on our own. Jesus deserved the blessing of God, but instead He took all of our sins upon Himself, and gave us His holiness and goodness in exchange. The Apostle Peter put it this way:

Who his own self bare our sins in his own body on the tree, that we, being dead to sins, should live unto righteousness: by whose stripes ye were healed.

1 Peter 2:24

Again, the Bible says of Jesus,

For he hath made him to be sin for us, who knew no sin; that we might be made the righteousness of God in him.

2 Corinthians 5:21

Jesus bore our sin, not His sin. He didn't have any sin to bear. He took our sin and paid the debt we couldn't pay. Jesus briefly became what we were—separated from God—so that we could become what He is: a son of God, accepted and in right relationship with Him. Jesus took all of our sin and gave us all of His righteousness.

No other religion in the world understands this. In other religions, the burden is on the worshiper to earn relationship, or right standing, with their god. True Christianity is the only religion on the face of the earth that has a Savior. Jesus came and saved us because we couldn't save ourselves. He paid the debt that we couldn't pay. It is beyond man's ability to even conceive of such a thing. Human beings could never come up with this concept of God becoming a man and suffering the punishment that we deserve.

Our acceptance with God isn't based on how holy we are; it's based on the sacrifice Jesus made for us. This is the *nearly-too-good-to-be-true* news of the Gospel of Jesus Christ.

I was raised in a Christian home. I was born again when I was eight years old, and I immediately began to hear the Word of

69

God. Because of those things, I lived a holy life from a young age. I have never used a word of profanity in all of my sixty years. I've never taken a drink of liquor. I've never smoked a cigarette. (I've never even tasted coffee, though there is a scripture that says you can drink any deadly thing and it shall not harm you - Mark 16:18 - so you can drink coffee. I'm just kidding, there's nothing wrong with drinking coffee!) But seriously, I have lived a very holy life by religious standards.

Even though I have lived a holy life, I still couldn't save myself. I may not have committed the so-called "cardinal sins" that religion teaches against, but I've been selfish. I've lied. I've been unfaithful to God. I haven't kept my word to people. I've made mistakes. Just like everyone else, I have come short of the glory of God, and the payment for my sin is death (Romans 6:23).

A lot of people today don't understand that being a good person, or living a holy life, won't save you. They think that if you're a good person, you're going to be okay. But being good isn't *good enough*. God's standard of holiness is impossible for us to achieve. We may look good compared to other people (2 Corinthians 10:12), but this is no comparison to the holiness of God. Jesus was the express image of God's glory and of His purpose (Hebrews 1:3). Jesus is God's standard for holiness, as He never committed a single sin, of commission or omission, in thought or deed, from birth until death. There is no such thing as "almost perfect." Either you're perfect or you aren't, and we aren't—that's why we need a Savior.

Paul began his letter to the Romans by saying that he wasn't ashamed of the Gospel of Christ because it is "the power of God unto salvation" (Romans 1:16). Your own efforts can never save you, but simply believing in Jesus will. The Gospel, or Good News, is that the burden of salvation is not on our shoulders, and we don't have to do anything to earn it.

Salvation includes deliverance from sin *and* its effects. If you don't have power working in you for healing, you don't really understand the Gospel. Satan is probably condemning you and making you feel unworthy. You believe God can heal, but you aren't convinced He wants to heal you because you think you are unworthy. You are still tying the display of God's power in your life to some worth or value on your part. You're trying to barter with God by saying, "Lord if You heal me, I'll start living a holy life. I'll do whatever You want me to." See, that's not approaching God on the basis of what Jesus has done. You aren't coming through the Gospel. You haven't accepted the nearly-too-good-to-be-true news that salvation, healing, and deliverance don't depend on your goodness. Jesus has already earned everything for you; all you have to do is believe!

> *For by grace are ye saved through faith; and that not of yourselves: it is the gift of God: not of works, lest any man should boast.*
> *Ephesians 2:8-9*

God has already provided everything by grace. It has nothing to do with our own holiness. Your actions don't determine whether God's power is released in your life. All you have to do is receive by faith what God has already provided. Not only salvation, but whatever you need from the Lord is available if you will simply believe the good news, the Gospel of Christ Jesus. We are saved, healed, made whole, and delivered by the grace of God.

Additional Resources:

1.*The Gospel: The Power of God* is a four-part audio teaching discussing grace and the book of Romans. It is available to listen to or download for free at http://www.awmi.net/extra/audio/1014

2.*Grace, the Power of the Gospel* book by Andrew Wommack shows that it isn't what you do, but what Christ did that makes you righteous. Never again worry if you are meeting God's holy standard. It is available through bookstores or the online store at http://www.awmi.net/store/usa/books/322

3."The Grace of Giving" is an audio teaching that shows how grace relates to giving. It is available to listen to or download for free at http://www.awmi.net/extra/audio/o04

4."Grace and Faith in Giving" is an audio teaching that shows us how to trust God with our finances. It is available to listen to or download for free at http://www.awmi.net/extra/audio/o14

God's Kind of Love: The Cure for What Ails Ya! is a three-part audio teaching that talks about how much God loves us. We can't give what we haven't received. Before we can love others, we have to have a true revelation of God's love for us. This series will help you receive a deeper revelation of God's unconditional love for you. It is available to listen to or download for free at http://www.awmi.net/extra/audio/1015

Chapter 8

Living in the Balance of Grace and Faith

The body of believers is mostly divided into two camps: those who believe that salvation and the gifts of God are received through faith, and those who think that everything is given by the grace of God. I believe the Word of God teaches that we receive from God through a combination of grace and faith, not one or the other.

> *For by grace are ye saved through faith; and that not of yourselves: it is the gift of God: not of works, lest any man should boast.*
>
> *Ephesians 2:8-9*

As this scripture says, we are saved *by grace through faith.* Those who hold fast to an extreme view of faith or grace are out of balance. This is similar to the chemicals sodium and chlorine: each on its own is a poison, but combined they yield table salt—something we can't live without. Faith or grace by themselves will poison you, but putting faith in God's grace is the path to life.

I need to define what I mean by "grace" and "faith," because they have become religious terms with varying definitions. Grace is what God does for you independent of what you deserve. God's grace has nothing to do with you. The Greek word that we translate "grace" in the Bible literally means unearned, undeserved favor—but it's even more than that. Grace is something God did for you prior to you having a need for it. God extended His grace to you before you even existed.

God's grace came to earth through Jesus 2,000 years ago (John 1:17). When Jesus died upon the cross, He died for all sin, for all time: past, present, and future (Hebrews 9:12). Jesus paid for our sin 2,000 years before we were born. God didn't look down and say, "They're such wonderful people, and they are trying so hard. I think I'll do something to help them." No, God anticipated our human state and our sin, and He paid the price before we were alive. Before the problem had come into existence, God had created the solution. That is grace.

If you had to be worthy in order to get God's grace, then it wouldn't be grace; it would be a payment you earned in exchange for your own goodness. God's grace is given independent of you. Grace is all God.

The danger is when people apply God's grace across the board and interpret it to mean that *everything* is up to God. From this viewpoint, God controls all things: who gets saved, who gets healed, who you marry, and on down to the finest details of life. But the Word of God teaches differently. For example, the Word says,

For the grace of God that bringeth salvation hath appeared to all men.

Titus 2:11

If salvation was purely up to God, and if grace alone saved, then all men would be saved—because God's grace has appeared to all men. God's grace was extended prior to your existence and it has nothing to do with you, so if grace by itself was sufficient for salvation, you would already be saved when you are born. No further action on your part would be required. But we aren't saved by grace alone. We're saved by grace through faith (Ephesians 2:8). It isn't up to God whether or not you get saved:

> *The Lord is not slack concerning his promise, as some men count slackness; but is longsuffering to us-ward, not willing that any should perish, but that all should come to repentance.*
> *2 Peter 3:9*

God desires that everyone be saved, but not everyone will be because it isn't God's decision to make. Salvation comes by the grace of God, but you have to respond with faith. Grace is God's part—faith is ours. It is faith in God's grace that releases the power of salvation in a person. Everything is available by the grace of God, but there has to be a faith response on our part to receive what is available by grace.

Before defining what faith is, I want to talk about what faith is not. Faith is not something you do to get God to respond to you or to act on your behalf. Anything you will ever need has already been provided by grace, including salvation, healing, deliverance, joy, peace, and prosperity. It's true that faith will cause the power of God to come into manifestation, but this isn't because God is responding to our faith. Faith doesn't move God. It moves us into position to receive what God has already provided by grace.

Faith is simply our positive response to God's grace.

It took me 20 years to understand those few words. Faith doesn't cause a positive response from God. God has already provided all things by grace. Faith is just your positive response to what God has already provided. Another way of saying it is that faith only appropriates what God has already provided by grace. If God hasn't already provided it independent of your efforts and prior to your need, then your faith can't make it happen.

Grace alone is poisonous, as is faith alone. One extreme is to believe that everything is determined by God's grace. The other is to believe that the faith of the believer controls every outcome. Consider this scripture:

> *For verily I say unto you, That whosoever shall say unto this mountain, Be thou removed, and be thou cast into the sea; and shall not doubt in his heart, but shall believe that those things which he saith shall come to pass; he shall have whatsoever he saith. Therefore I say unto you, What things soever ye desire, when ye pray, believe that ye receive them, and ye shall have them.*
>
> *Mark 11:23-24*

This scripture says whatever things you desire, when you pray, believe that you receive them and you will have them. People who take an extreme view of faith have misinterpreted this to indicate that they can have whatever they want—provided they have the faith to believe for it. This misunderstanding of faith has led some to have false expectations of what is possible by faith, sometimes with bizarre results.

Living in the Balance of Grace and Faith

I remember a woman in Arlington, Texas, who was in the extreme faith camp and was teaching its message to her students at a Bible school she opened. She took this scripture from Mark 11 that says you can have "whatsoever ye desire," and decided she wanted Kenneth Copeland (a well known minister) as her husband. The problem was that he was already married to Gloria Copeland. So, this woman held a mock wedding where she married Kenneth "in the spirit," and then "stood in faith" waiting for Gloria to die and get out of her way so she could unite with Kenneth.

Most people would recognize there is something wrong with this picture. "Whatsoever ye desire" isn't a free ticket to receive by faith anything that strikes your fancy. *Faith only appropriates what God has already provided by grace.* God didn't provide murder and adultery through the atonement of Jesus, so you can't believe for someone to die in order to take their spouse.

Some people have this concept that they are going to grab hold of God and not let go until He gives them what they want. They say, "I'm going to make God heal so-and-so," "I'm going to make God prosper me," or "I'm going to make my spouse stay with me." But faith doesn't make God do anything. If it wasn't provided for in the atonement of Jesus, your faith can't make it happen. All faith does is reach out and partake of what God has already provided by grace.

When God created Adam and Eve, He created everything they would ever need. Not only did God anticipate their needs, but He anticipated the needs of all the people who would ever live on the face of the earth. God created this world with enough oxygen to sustain Adam and Eve, and as many descendants as would ever

77

exist on this planet. He created enough food to feed all of earth's inhabitants. There's a reason Adam and Eve weren't created until the sixth day: if God had created them first, they would have had to tread water for two days until there was land to stand on. And then they would have had to dodge the mountains and trees as they sprung up from the earth. God anticipated everything.

God created all things and, by grace, He provided for all of the needs that Adam and Eve would ever have. Still, their needs weren't automatically fulfilled. Adam and Eve had a part to play. They had to reach out and partake of God's grace. God provided fruit to eat, for instance, but they had to take it and eat. The Lord didn't create them with a tube into their stomach so they could be fed without any effort on their part. They had to gather and use what God had provided. If they had sat around waiting for God to spoon-feed them every meal, they would have starved to death.

In the same way, God has already provided everything we will ever need—that's grace—but we have to reach out and take it by faith.

You don't make God heal you. God has already provided for your healing through grace. What you do is reach out and take that healing by faith. Your faith doesn't make healing happen any more than Adam and Eve, by reaching out their arm, made a tree shoot from the ground and sprout fruit. The trees were already there, but Adam and Eve had to harvest the fruit. Likewise, we have a part to play in reaching out to obtain God's promises—our part is faith.

Believers in the extreme grace camp say that everything comes by the grace of God, and they don't see any role for themselves.

Their approach to life is *Que sera, sera,* whatever will be, will be. People with this attitude don't see the point in doing anything, or even seeking God, because they believe everything has already been determined by His grace. They end up floating lazily down the river of life, waiting to see what happens next.

Believers in the extreme faith camp recognize that we have a role to play, but they overemphasize that role. They understand that God's will doesn't automatically come to pass, so they focus on how important it is for the individual to do things (read the Word, pray, have faith, etc.). If you aren't careful, you can fall into believing that it is your own actions that are producing results. You can start to think that your goodness is making God move on your behalf, which leads to pride and Phariseeism.

Any time a truth from God's Word is taken to an extreme, or to the exclusion of other truths, it leads to error. Faith is poison by itself, and grace is poison by itself. But when you put faith in what God has already done by grace, it becomes a combination you can't live without. It's the balance of grace and faith, and it will release the power of God in your life.

Sharper than a Two-Edged Sword

Additional Resources:

1.*Living in the Balance of Grace and Faith* is a five-part audio teaching available to listen to or download for free at http://www.awmi.net/extra/audio/1064

2.*Living in the Balance of Grace and Faith* book by Andrew Wommack gives a correct understanding of grace and faith and how they work together. In this book, Andrew clearly explains both concepts and how living in the balance of the two will change your relationship with God forever. It is available through bookstores or the online store at http://www.awmi.net/store/usa/books/228

3.*Insights into Faith* is a small book by Andrew Wommack that consists of a compilation of footnotes from the Life for Today Study Bible on the subject of faith. These notes have been organized and tied together to produce a powerful 52-page book that will build your faith. It is available through the online store at http://www.awmi.net/store/usa/books/100 "The Faith of God" is an audio teaching that discusses the difference between human faith and spiritual faith. It is available to listen to or download for free at http://www.awmi.net/extra/audio/a01

Chapter 9

The Believer's Authority

W hen a room in your house goes dark, you don't call the electric company and ask them to turn on the lights—you turn them on yourself. Electric companies supply the power, but it's up to you to flip the light switch and put that power to use. Similarly, I believe that the number one reason for unanswered prayer is that people are asking God to do something that He has given us the power and authority to do for ourselves. Asking God to do things He told us to do isn't going to bring answers to our prayers. Christians generally don't understand the authority that God has given them. The average person is approaching God as if they have no power or authority. I've had hundreds of people come to me with tears in their eyes, present their problem to me, and basically tell me they are powerless to change their situation. Yet believers are anything but powerless. Starting from a position of powerlessness is completely contrary to everything that the Word of God teaches.

Jesus gave His disciples the power to cast out demons and to heal all manner of sickness (Matthew 10:1). He also gave them the authority to use that power, and He commanded them to use it, saying,

*And as ye go, preach, saying, The kingdom of heaven is at hand.
Heal the sick, cleanse the lepers, raise the dead, cast out devils:
freely ye have received, freely give.*

Matthew 10:7-8

Jesus said, "Heal the sick." He didn't say *pray* for the sick. It may seem a subtle difference, but in practice it makes an enormous difference. A large segment of Christians don't even believe that God heals today because they never see anything happen when they pray. They don't look for supernatural manifestations of God's power. Even among those who do believe in the miraculous power of God, a large portion aren't following the model Jesus put forth. Instead, they are starting from a position of powerlessness, saying things like, "Lord, we are nothing. We can do nothing. We're just waiting on You. God, stretch forth Your hand and heal." They are pleading and begging with God to release His power, which is completely contrary to Jesus' command.

Jesus gave us power over all sickness, disease, and demons. Then He said, "Now, you heal the sick, cast out devils, cleanse the lepers, and raise the dead." He didn't tell us to pray and ask Him to do it for us. He told us to go out and to do these things. We aren't doing it on our own, because it's God's power working the miracle, but we are responsible for taking action. The Lord said,

I am the vine, ye are the branches: He that abideth in me, and I in him, the same bringeth   forth much fruit: for without me ye can do nothing.

John 15:5

The Believer's Authority

Without Jesus, I am a zero with the rim knocked off. On my own, I can't heal a gnat—but I'm never on my own. The Lord has promised that He will never leave us nor forsake us (Hebrews 13:5). After you are born again, God places His power on the inside of you—power over all sickness and disease, and over every demon. Since we already have God's power and the authority to use it, we don't have to ask Him to heal the sick or cast out demons for us.

The same power that raised Christ from the dead is now dwelling in us (Ephesians 1:19-20). Whenever you approach God as if you are powerless to change your situation, you reveal that you don't understand the power that He has given you. You might be asking for the right thing or seeking the right results, but you're going about it in the wrong way. Miracles don't come to pass that way. The Scripture says,

> *Submit yourselves therefore to God. Resist the devil, and he will flee from you.*
>
> *James 4:7*

God told us to resist the devil and the devil will flee from us. The word "resist" means to actively fight against. It is our responsibility to resist the devil. You can't go to God and ask Him to get the devil off of your back; you have to fight against the devil yourself.

Sickness and disease are works of the devil (John 10:10), so when we ask God to heal our sicknesses we are, in effect, asking Him to rebuke the devil for us. But God told us to resist the devil. If we don't resist the devil, he won't go away. I can beg and plead with God until I'm blue in the face—I can give Him all the ins-and-outs of how desperate my situation is—but nothing is going to happen until I resist the devil myself.

It's God's power, but it's our responsibility to put it to use.

A lot of people don't like to hear this because it makes us accountable, and we have become masters at dodging responsibility. We'll find any reason to put the blame on someone or something else: upbringing, ethnicity, lack of education, parents, abuse, or anything else we can think of. We try to cope with our own failures by placing the blame elsewhere. I'm not saying that bad things don't happen to people, but until you take responsibility for your own actions, you'll never be more than a victim. To be a victor, you have to take responsibility. God has given you the power to change your situation if you will quit being a victim and stand up and resist the devil.

I heard a story about a vision that Kenneth Hagin had. In the vision, Kenneth was standing in front of the Lord, and He was saying some important things to Kenneth. In the midst of their conversation, a demon ran right in front of Kenneth and started making all sorts of noise so that Kenneth was having a hard time hearing what the Lord was saying. As Kenneth strained to hear, he was wondering why the Lord didn't tell the demon to go away. In frustration, Kenneth finally yelled at the little demon to leave in the name of Jesus. At his command, the demon fled. The Lord then told Kenneth that He did not tell the demon to flee because it was Kenneth's responsibility. The Lord said to him, "I have given you the authority, and I can't take it back."

The point of this story is consistent with what is revealed in the Word of God. The Bible says that when something comes out of the mouth of the Lord, it's a covenant. God said,

My covenant will I not break, nor alter the thing that is gone out of my lips.

Psalm 89:34

When God says something, it's binding to Him. People, by contrast, will say anything on a whim and then change their minds later. Even when something is in writing, people hire lawyers to get around agreements they have made. Words might not mean much to people, but God never violates His word. The Bible says of Jesus,

Who being the brightness of his glory, and the express image of his person, and upholding all things by the word of his power, when he had by himself purged our sins, sat down on the right hand of the Majesty on high.

Hebrews 1:3

Jesus was a perfect, identical representation of the Father, and He upholds all things by the word of His power. This universe is held together by the power of Jesus' words. If Jesus ever violated the integrity of His word, then things would cease to be held together and the universe would be destroyed. It isn't an option for God to tell us to do something and then to go back on His word and do it for us.

God wants you well, but He will not violate His word to heal you. God told us to resist the devil, and if we don't do it —for whatever reason—He isn't going to do it for us. He gave us raising-from-the-dead power, but we have to believe and resist the devil.

The apostles Peter and John demonstrated this principle when they healed a lame man on their way to the Temple. The man had been lame from birth, and every day he sat by the Temple begging alms from those who were on their way in. As Peter and John approached him that day he asked for alms,

> *And Peter, fastening his eyes upon him with John, said, Look on us. And he gave heed unto them, expecting to receive something of them. Then Peter said, Silver and gold have I none; but such as I have give I thee: In the name of Jesus Christ of Nazareth rise up and walk.*
>
> *Acts 3:4-6*

Peter took hold of the lame man's hand and stood him up. Immediately, the lame man was healed and went leaping before them, praising God for the miracle he received. This is an awesome demonstration of the power of God, but notice that Peter and John never prayed for the man. They didn't ask God to heal him, and they didn't start from a position of powerlessness by saying that they were nothing and could do nothing. Peter said, "What I have I give to you." He wasn't being arrogant. Jesus told Peter that he had the healing power of God, and Peter was just putting it to use.

As a whole, the body of Christ isn't using the authority that God has given us—often, because we don't know what we have. Many in the Church are begging and pleading with God to move, but they don't believe that God has already moved. God has already given us the power and authority to speak to our problems.

Fig trees are unique fruit trees because they produce fruit at the same time that they leaf out. So, when a fig tree is full of green leaves, it should have fruit as well. Scripture records that one day, Jesus saw from a distance a fig tree with leaves and walked to it, wanting to find food. When He got to the tree, it didn't have any fruit. It looked like it had fruit on it, but it didn't. It was emblematic of religious hypocrisy. The tree was professing to possess something that it didn't really have. Seeing this, Jesus cursed the fig tree. The next day, Jesus and His disciples walked by the tree and it was dead. It had dried up from the roots (Mark 11:20).

The moment Jesus spoke to the tree it died, but it took twenty-four hours for what had happened to become visible. This is important to remember when you pray. The effects of prayer are not always immediately evident to our senses, but power always goes forth when we pray in the name of Jesus. If we wait patiently in faith, expecting to see what we pray for, then we will see it come to pass. As the disciples passed by the dried up fig tree, Peter pointed out to Jesus that it had died:

And Jesus answering saith unto them, Have faith in God. For verily I say unto you, That whosoever shall say unto this mountain, Be thou removed, and be thou cast into the sea; and shall not doubt in his heart, but shall believe that those things which he saith shall come to pass; he shall have whatsoever he saith. Therefore I say unto you, What things soever ye desire, when ye pray, believe that ye receive them, and ye shall have them.

Mark 11:22-24

Three times in this passage, the Lord emphasizes the power of words. Jesus didn't touch the fig tree or try to pull it down; He just spoke to it. All that is necessary to release the faith and power that

87

God has given you is to speak to your problem. Faith and power are released through words. Jesus said, whosoever shall say, and believe the things he says, will have whatsoever he says. Words are powerful. Proverbs says,

> *Death and life are in the power of the tongue: and they that love it shall eat the fruit thereof.*
>
> *Proverbs 18:21*

The miracle you are waiting for is in your mouth—if you would speak and not doubt. The problem is that most of us say things that we don't believe with our whole heart. We waver, and the Bible says that those who waver don't receive anything from God (James 1:6-8). Jesus said that when we pray, we have to believe and not doubt in our hearts. We can't waver. We have to speak and believe.

Also notice that Jesus instructed us to speak to the mountain. It's important to recognize that when you have an obstacle in your way or a problem, you need to *speak directly to the problem.* Most Christians spend ten minutes describing the problem, and the next ten seconds begging God to make it go away. "O God," they cry, "please move this mountain." But that is a totally wrong approach. God didn't tell us to talk to Him about our problems and ask Him to make them go away. He told us to speak to the mountain and cast it into the sea.

For you to speak to your mountain and command it to get out of the way implies that you understand God has already done His part. He gave you power and authority. Instead of speaking to God as if you can do nothing, you need to believe that God has given you (past tense) power and authority. Now, take your authority and resist the situation. You speak and command the mountain to get out of your way. You talk to it! In other words, talk to your problem about God; don't talk to God about your problem.

I believe that in the vast majority of churches, though not all, religion doesn't emphasize the authority of the believer because it's a safe way to play it. If you don't have any authority, you don't have to hold yourself accountable. You can go to a person who is dying and throw out a half-hearted prayer, and if nothing happens it isn't your fault. It's easy to live your life that way. People blame God and say, "It must not have been His will to heal this time." That isn't true. It isn't always as simple as praying for someone and seeing them healed because the person you are praying for needs to be in agreement, but it is always God's will to heal.

Instead of asking God to heal, praise Him that He has already provided healing. Don't tell God about your problem; speak to your problem about God. Say, "Cancer, in the name of Jesus, I command you to get out of my body." That is exactly what Jesus instructed us to do: speak to our mountain (Mark 11:23).

I once prayed for a woman who had severe pain throughout her body. The pain had been present for seven years, and the date that doctors predicted she would die had passed three years before I even met her. She was in terrible shape. I explained to her the source of the believers' authority and the need to speak directly to her problem, and then I prayed with her. She was instantly healed and started praising God.

After she was healed, I spent another twenty minutes teaching her to not quit believing that God healed her. Feeling a symptom of illness after you have prayed doesn't mean you weren't healed. It's like the fig tree that dried up from the roots: sometimes it takes a little time to see the healing fully manifest to your senses. Also, the devil is going to probe to see if you really believed when you prayed. He'll come with symptoms, like a knock at your door, to see if you'll open up and let him back in. The devil wants to see if he can get you to back off of believing that God healed you. One of the ways he does it is by bringing back symptoms or thoughts that remind you of being sick. If you ever have another pain or symptom, just speak to it. Believe that God has given you power, then resist the pain or sickness and it will flee from you.

When we were done talking, the woman started to leave, but as soon as she touched the doorknob to open the door, the stinging pain returned. I reminded her that I had just spent twenty minutes teaching her what to do, and I told her that I would agree with her as she prayed.

She said, "I claim my healing, in the name of Jesus. By Your stripes I was healed." She prayed for a little while longer, and she said some good things, but she didn't take her authority and speak directly to the problem.

"Do you still have any stinging?" I asked her.

"Yes," she said.

"Do you know why?" I asked.

"No," she replied.

"It's because you didn't talk to the stinging," I told her. "You talked to God and confessed your faith in God, but you didn't take your authority and speak to the problem."

"You mean I'm supposed to say, 'stinging be gone in the name of Jesus'?"

"Exactly," I said.

We joined hands to pray again and she said, "Stinging, in Jesus' name…"

That's as far as she got before the stinging fled her body. It's been eight years or so and she has been totally free of that problem ever since.

Many believers are doing exactly what that woman did: saying good things, but not taking the authority God has given them and using it. Peter said, "Such as I have," and he commanded the lame man to be well. God has placed His power and authority on the inside of us, but it is our responsibility to use it. Once you begin to use what God has given you instead of asking Him to do it for you, you will see a dramatic change in the results you get when you pray.

Additional Resources:

1. *The Believer's Authority* is a six-part audio teaching available to listen to or download for free at http://www.awmi.net/extra/audio/1045

2. *The Believer's Authority* book by Andrew Wommack reveals the spiritual significance of your choices, words, and actions and how they affect your ability to stand against the attacks of Satan and receive God's best. Discover the powerful truths behind true spiritual authority and begin seeing real results. It is available through bookstores or the online store at http://www.awmi.net/store/usa/books/327

3. *Don't Limit God* is an empowering five-part audio teaching that reveals how we limit God in our lives, and what we can do to break free from our self-imposed limitations. It is available to listen to or download for free at http://www.awmi.net/extra/audio/1060 Spiritual Authority is a six-part audio teaching that takes the cover off Satan's deception and shows us the power that God has committed to us. Watch your faith soar and your situation improve as you receive the truths of your spiritual authority in Christ. It is available to listen to or download for free at http://www.awmi.net/extra/audio/1017

Sharper than a Two-Edged Sword

Chapter 10

A Better Way to Pray

At one of my *Gospel Truth Seminars*, I asked anyone who believed in the power of prayer to raise their hand. Nearly every hand in the audience went up. Then I asked everyone who sees all of their prayers answered to keep their hands up. Just about every hand went right back down. It demonstrated a common problem among Christians today: very few people are seeing consistent answers to prayer. But the Bible teaches that everyone who seeks, finds and everyone who asks, receives:

> *Ask, and it shall be given you; seek, and ye shall find; knock, and it shall be opened unto you: For every one that asketh receiveth; and he that seeketh findeth; and to him that knocketh it shall be opened.*
>
> *Matthew 7:7-8*

Clearly, there's a problem somewhere—and we know it isn't with God. I believe that there is a better way for us to pray, a way that leads to finding what we seek and receiving what we ask. It's not the *only way* to pray, and God isn't mad at you if you pray differently. I just think there is a more effective way for us to pray that gets better results.

I should add that I have prayed in every way I'm about to advise you *not* to pray, so I'm not saying that you aren't saved unless you pray like I do now. I have prayed in a lot of "wrong" ways in the past, but I loved God and I was doing it with a pure heart. Over time, however, I have discovered that the Word of God teaches a better way to pray. By following it, I'm getting better results than I have ever gotten before.

When Jesus taught on prayer, He spent time identifying the wrong ways to pray. So, before I get into the *better* way to pray, I want to talk about what prayer is not. One of the first things Jesus taught His disciples about prayer was:

> *And when thou prayest, thou shalt not be as the hypocrites are: for they love to pray standing in the synagogues and in the corners of the streets, that they may be seen of men. Verily I say unto you, They have their reward.*
>
> *Matthew 6:5*

The Lord made a startling statement here: He said that hypocrites love to pray. Therefore prayer, in and of itself, is not that valuable. All of the world's religions pray. Some groups bow down on mats multiple times a day in prayer, and then they get up and go kill people in the name of God. They are devout, yet their life is contrary to everything that the true Word of God reveals. They are praying, but they aren't in contact with God. Unfortunately, there are also a lot of religious Christians who pray all of the time, but they aren't connecting with God. Prayer is no good unless you are connecting with God. Communication requires interaction, so God needs to be speaking back to you.

A Better Way to Pray

Prayer also needs to be real. I have heard people change their voice when they pray and start speaking Old English. "We beseech Thee," they say, "that Thou mightest, wouldest, couldest do thus and such." I suppose there might be cases where a person has heard prayers like that so many times that they think they have to talk that way in order to communicate with God, but usually it's just religious hypocrisy. God doesn't speak Old English. I use the *King James Version* Bible, but I don't pray in King James language. I don't prophesy to people in King James language.

Changing your voice or personality to talk with God isn't genuine prayer. God wants us to talk to Him like He is a real person. We need to drop all of the religious trappings. You don't have to have your hands folded with your eyes closed, and be in a kneeling position to pray. Those things may be appropriate at certain times, but they aren't required.

Prayer is just communication with God. Even meditation, or what you are thinking, can be prayer to God. Scripture says, "Give ear to my words, O LORD, consider my meditation. Hearken unto the voice of my cry, my King, and my God: for unto thee will I pray" (Psalm 5:1-2). Not all prayer needs to be spoken; it can be the meditation of your heart. When Jesus arrived at the tomb of Lazarus and was about to raise him from the dead, He said, "Father, I thank thee that thou hast heard me" (John 11:41), but He hadn't spoken a prayer yet. Apparently, Jesus had prayed in His heart. He was in constant communication with God, not just when He spoke.

Imagine going to your pastor for advice and upon arriving at his or her office, you immediately launch into a monologue that lasts for an hour. You never give the pastor the opportunity to give you any input whatsoever, and when the hour is finished you say, "Thank you," and walk out of the office. That wouldn't be very smart. The whole point of going to someone for advice is to hear what they have to say.

I had a very close friend who was a pastor, and we used to pray together. I remember he was telling me a story one time about how God had recently spoken to him while he was in the shower. My friend stopped in the middle of the story and said to me, "I wonder why God always talks to me in when I'm in the shower or out running? I pray for hours every day, and God never speaks to me when I'm praying. It's always when I'm in the shower or something that I get these revelations from God."

As soon as he asked the question, I thought to myself, *I know exactly why God doesn't talk to you when you pray.*

My friend's mouth was like a rapid-fire machine gun when he prayed. He'd start praying, *Bam, Bam, Bam,* and hardly stop to take a breath.

He wasn't getting revelation when he prayed because he never gave God an opportunity to say anything. The Lord couldn't get a word in edgewise. Prayer isn't effective if you don't let God speak.

Aside from talking too much, we tend to compartmentalize prayer into a separate time of our day. A man once came to my office and asked me how much I prayed. As I was considering the question and trying to quantify how much I prayed every day, the Lord spoke to me. My wife and I had spent the entire previous day together. We weren't talking the whole time, but we were together doing different things. We ate together, drove in the car together, and had a great day.

The Lord asked me, "How much time did you spend with Jamie yesterday?"

The whole day, I thought.

Then the Lord said, "I'm available twenty-four hours a day. Why reduce the time that you communicate with me down to thirty minutes or an hour?"

Jamie and I would have a sorry relationship if I ignored her when we were together eating dinner, driving in the car, and being in the same room without ever acknowledging that she was there. God is with us all the time. *We can spend the entire day in the presence of the Lord.* Instead of only setting aside certain times for prayer, we can be in communion with God constantly.

I have developed a lifestyle of keeping my mind focused on the Lord regardless of what I'm doing. Even when I'm busy making television programs, I'm still listening to the Lord. God speaks to me and reminds me of things and I'm constantly in communion with Him—that's what prayer is. Jesus said,

> But thou, when thou prayest, enter into thy closet, and when thou hast shut thy door, pray to thy Father which is in secret; and thy Father which seeth in secret shall reward thee openly.

> *Matthew 6:6*

Prayer is not supposed to be something we do for acclaim from other people. Someone who is trying to compare the amount of time he or she spends in prayer with the time that other people spend in prayer is praying for the wrong reasons. Merely spending time in prayer doesn't earn you extra favor with God. The motivation for prayer should be that we desire to have relationship and communion with God. Besides, Jesus made it very clear that length of time isn't what makes prayer good:

> *But when ye pray, use not vain repetitions, as the heathen do: for they think that they shall be heard for their much speaking.*
> *Matthew 6:7*

Some of the best prayers that you can utter are short ones, like *"Help!"* That's a great prayer. Jesus saw great miracles happen when He prayed, but He prayed short and to the point. "Peace, be still," calmed a raging storm. "Lazarus, come forth," was enough to raise the dead. Many times when we pray long extended prayers it's only because we're trying to psyche ourselves into believing. Short prayers actually take great faith. Jesus said that we are not going to be heard based on how long we pray because the quality of a prayer is much more important than its quantity.

The disciples asked Jesus to teach them to pray, and He taught them a model that has become known as "The Lord's Prayer" (Matthew 6:9-13). It starts off by praising God, which is consistent with what is written in the Psalms where it says, "Enter into His gates with thanksgiving, and into His courts with praise: be thankful unto him, and bless his name" (Psalm 100:4). It also ends with praise, and in the middle is a request to "give us this day our daily bread." It's a great model for prayer, but it was never intended to be recited the way it is by so many Christians today. There may be some benefit to reciting it, but that's missing the point. Jesus only offered it as a *way* to pray. It shows you that you enter into His gates with thanksgiving, slip in your prayer request, and then finish by praising God.

Rote memorization and recitation of prayers is vain repetition. If you look at some of the groups who pray multiple times a day at specific times, they are just going through a ritual and chanting a mantra. There is no communion with God. I'm saying this with love, but merely praying the rosary and reciting a canned "Our Father" style prayer is a form of vain repetition. Jesus said the heathen pray like that, but we shouldn't. God wants relationship with us. We shouldn't make prayer so structured that we don't have any true communion with Him.

I also need to point out that there is a huge difference between the way people prayed under the Old Covenant, and the way that we pray under the New Covenant. For instance, after David was caught in adultery and the murder of Bathsheba's husband was brought to light, David prayed:

> *Create in me a clean heart, O God; and renew a right spirit within me. Cast me not away from thy presence; and take not thy holy spirit from me.*
> *Psalm 51:10-11*

It was appropriate for David to pray those words because he wasn't born again, but under the New Covenant it is wrong for us to ask God to create in us a clean heart or renew our spirit. God gave you a clean heart when you were born again, and you can't ever lose that clean heart. Your body and your mind may be defiled, but your born-again spirit is sealed by the Holy Spirit and it always retains relationship with God (Ephesians 1:13).

The prayers being spoken today are often completely contrary to the Word of God. People are beginning church services by saying, "O God, please be with us as we meet today," when God has promised that He will never leave you nor forsake you (Hebrews 13:5). Prayers like that demonstrate a lack of understanding of what really happened to us when we were born again. We became entirely new creatures: old things passed away, all things became new, and we were made the righteousness of God in Christ Jesus (2 Corinthians 5:17). We don't need to approach God through a mediator as they did in the Old Covenant, and we don't need to ask God to make us worthy. Jesus made us worthy.

Another wrong concept of prayer being promoted today at "spiritual warfare" conferences is the idea that you have to get your prayers past demonic opposition in the heavens for God to receive them. The whole notion that you have to create a hole in the heavens so your prayers can reach God is completely wrong. Every born-again believer is the temple of the Holy Spirit (1 Corinthians 6:19). God lives in you, so you don't need your prayer to get above your nose. It is true that we have an enemy, but the devil can't stop you from communicating with God.

Like I said, at one time or another, I have done everything that I have just taught here is wrong. When I was first really turned on to the Lord, I wanted to spend more time focused on God in prayer, so I came up with a routine. I would pray from seven to nine every morning. I would stop whatever I was doing and pray for an hour or two. I did it as a discipline to focus on God, and there was probably some benefit to it, but after a while I started to dread that time. I would pray for about five minutes and think half an hour had gone by. I just didn't know how to pray. I wasn't connecting with God. I was talking a lot, but I'm not sure that I was listening. It was just a monologue, and it became ritualistic.

One morning as it was getting close to seven o'clock, I said to the Lord, "God, I hate to admit this, but you know my heart anyway: I dread this prayer time. I start dreading it at 6:45," I said.

"Andrew," the Lord said to me, "don't feel bad. I start dreading it at 6."

I thought, *If God isn't enjoying it, and I'm not enjoying it, then why am I doing it?* I realized it was just a religious exercise. It was something I was doing to make myself feel holy, but I wasn't connecting with God.

The purpose of prayer is simply relationship with God—it is fellowship and communion with Him. There are times when we have to use the authority God has given us and command sickness or obstacles to flee, but mostly prayer is about building relationship with God. It is an opportunity for us to spend time with our Heavenly Father, and to be further transformed into His image.

God is always present, and the blood of Jesus has made it possible for us to enter into the Holy of Holies (Hebrews 10:19). The veil has been torn in two, and the obstacles that separated mankind from God under the Old Covenant have been removed. Now, we can enter boldly into the throne room of God and soak in His presence.

Additional Resources:

1.*A Better Way to Pray* is a five-part audio teaching available to listen to or download for free at http://www.awmi.net/extra/audio/1042

2.*A Better Way to Pray* book by Andrew Wommack addresses a better way to pray if you're not getting the results you desire. It is available through bookstores or the online store at http://www.awmi.net/store/usa/books/321

3. *How to Become a Water Walker: Lessons in Faith* is a five-part audio teaching available to listen to or download for free at http://www.awmi.net/extra/audio/1037

4.*How to Find God's Will* is a five-part audio teaching available to listen to or download for free at http://www.awmi.net/extra/audio/1066

5.How to Follow God's Will is a five-part audio teaching available to listen to or download for free at http://www.awmi.net/extra/audio/1067

6.*How to Fulfill God's Will* is a five-part audio teaching available to listen to or download for free at http://www.awmi.net/extra/audio/1068

Hebrews Highlights is a five-part audio teaching that teaches the difference in our approach to prayer under the New Covenant versus the Old Covenant. Most believers haven't understood the difference; they still mix the old with the new, and it's the reason they aren't victorious. Hebrews was written to address this issue. This teaching is available to listen to or download for free at http://www.awmi.net/extra/audio/1061

Chapter 11

The Effects of Praise

You can check a person's spiritual pulse by examining how thankful they are. The amount of time you spend praising God is the greatest single indicator of where you are in your relationship with the Lord. Anyone who isn't praising God and operating in thanksgiving—regardless of what is going on in their life—doesn't really understand what God has done for them. Most people are content to praise God when things are going well, but their praise stops when the stress of life starts pressing in. Yet times of conflict are when we should be praising God the most. Praise builds your faith, runs off the devil, and ministers to God.

Praise shouldn't be the caboose that follows along the circumstances in your life. It should be the engine driving your life. Praise will take you places. It will change your circumstances. Scripture says,

> *As ye have therefore received Christ Jesus the Lord, so walk ye in him: Rooted and built up in him, and established in the faith, as ye have been taught, abounding therein with thanksgiving.*
>
> *Colossians 2:6-7*

Notice that we abound in faith through thanksgiving. Praise is a high form of faith. During difficult trials, abounding in faith includes praising God as you wait for the manifestation of His power to bring you through. Praise causes faith to thrive, and numerous scriptures say we should give thanks in every situation. For instance,

> *I will bless the LORD at all times: his praise shall continually be in my mouth.*
>
> *Psalm 34:1*

This verse doesn't say praise God when you feel like it, or when things are going great. It says to praise at *all times*. The Word tells us to praise God because it makes us focus on what God says rather than on our problems. If the doctor tells you that you are terminally ill, remember that the Word says to give thanks in all circumstances. Start praising God, and it will redirect your attention to God's will for you and build your faith to receive a miracle.

Your life is going in the direction of your dominant thoughts (Proverbs 23:7). Whatever you think about and focus your attention on determines the course of your life. Thoughts that focus on the circumstances around you only lead to discouragement. Focusing on your circumstances is only going to hinder faith. Praise, on the other hand, will establish you in faith. It will draw on God's power and allow you to receive the provision that Jesus purchased for you on the cross.

Praising God doesn't mean you say, "Thank You, Father, that I've only got six months to live. Praise You that I'm going to die." It means you look beyond your problem to the promises in God's

The Effects of Praise

Word and say, "Thank You, Father, that even though the doctor says I'm sick, Your Word says 'I shall not die, but live, and declare the works of the LORD' (Ps. 118:17). Your Word says that You wish above all things that I prosper and be in health even as my soul prospers (3 John 2). By Your stripes I was healed (1 Peter 2:24)." As you praise God and focus on His Word, it will turn your attention to the promise instead of the problem. Focusing on the Word builds your faith because faith comes by hearing (Romans 10:17).

Faith is the assurance of what you are hoping for, and the conviction that it has happened—even if you can't feel it or see it (Hebrews 11:1). Think about that for a moment. How would you respond if you were believing God for one million dollars, and I walked up to you and handed you a check for that amount? If you knew my check was good, and believed it was the answer to your prayer, you would celebrate. One person might jump and shout. Someone else might begin to cry. Another would fall to their knees and lift their hands to Jesus. It would differ from person to person, but there would be some response of praise. In the same way, faith isn't complete until it is mixed with praise.

If you aren't praising God—even before you see the physical manifestation of what you are believing for—then your faith isn't complete. You haven't yet abounded in faith. I really can't overemphasize how important praise is to faith.

I've had bad circumstances pop up in my life, and I have praised my way through them. During difficult times, I focus on God and think, *What's the worst thing that could happen?* The worst thing would be that I die—but if I die, I get to go be with the Lord. I start thinking about how, in heaven, there is no more sorrow and no more pain. I won't have any problems in heaven. As you think about the promises of God, it shrinks the problem you're facing down to a manageable size. It takes huge issues that look like mountains, and reduces them into tiny little anthills you can step right over. Suddenly, you'll realize the problem you are facing is no big deal.

Praise powerfully affects the believer, but it is also a weapon against the devil. When Jesus entered into Jerusalem upon a donkey in the days before He was crucified, people lined the way and laid palm branches on the path before Him, shouting, "Hosanna to the Son of David." The crowds followed Jesus all the way to the Temple and continued to praise Him. When the chief priests and the scribes heard the things that were being said, they asked Him, "Do you hear what they are saying?" Jesus answered them,

> *Yea; have ye never read, Out of the mouth of babes and sucklings thou hast perfected praise?*
>
> *Matthew 21:16*

He was quoting from an Old Testament passage, which says,

> *Out of the mouth of babes and sucklings hast thou ordained strength because of thine enemies, that thou mightest still the enemy and the avenger.*
>
> *Psalm 8:2*

These two scriptures together show us that *praise is strength to still the enemy and the avenger.* The reason for this has to do with why Satan transgressed against God in the first place. Isaiah the prophet tells us that Satan was envious of God because he wanted for himself the praise that God was receiving (Isaiah 14:13-14). Pride made Satan want to be like God. I believe the reason that praise affects the devil so powerfully is because when we praise God, it rubs the devil's nose in what he has always wanted but will never get. It's like taunting the devil, and it infuriates him.

We've all known self-centered people who think that life revolves around them. They need all the attention, and if they aren't the center of the conversation, it upsets them. It's an attitude that comes from the devil. Satan is the most egocentric personality in the universe. He is jealous of God, and when you start giving God praise, it drives the devil crazy. He can't stand to hear God praised. It makes him mad, and he flees.

Praising God puts to flight all of the hurts, pains, and demonic oppression with which Satan has tried to bind you. It opens up your heart and prepares you to receive from God. One of the classic examples of this is when Paul and Silas were beaten and thrown into prison in Philippi. After whipping them, the jailer threw them in the inner dungeon and put their feet in stocks. At midnight, Paul and Silas began to pray and sing praises unto God (Acts 16:25). Suddenly, there was a great earthquake and all of the prisoners' doors opened and their chains dropped off.

When the miracle came, Paul and Silas didn't quit praising God and they didn't run out of the prison. The jailer assumed everyone had escaped and was about to take his own life, but Paul called out for him to stop because all of the prisoners were still there. The greatest miracle here is that none of the other criminals fled. They were so affected by the praise and the power of God that they would rather stay in prison where the anointing of God was, than take advantage of the situation to flee.

This shows that Paul and Silas didn't praise God just to get out of their chains. They praised God because they were in love with Him. Their love for God drove them to praise Him—even though their backs were bleeding and they had been thrown in prison unjustly. Praise is powerful, and it releases the anointing of God. God inhabits the praises of his people (Psalm 22:3), and when you start praising God, it draws the power and the anointing of the Lord into manifestation. Praise will break your chains, it will drive the devil off, and get you out of bad situations.

Still, praise has another, more important benefit: it blesses God. It's a way for us to give back to Him.

God is the Almighty, but that doesn't mean we can't do something that ministers to Him. Jesus had needs while He was on earth, and many people ministered to Him by doing things such as cooking and caring for Him. God is love (1 John 4:8), and love likes to be reciprocated. God loved us so much that He gave His only Son to die for us, to bring us back into proper relationship with Him (John 3:16). Our praise is a thanksgiving that lets God know how much we appreciate what He has done for us. It reciprocates the love that He first loved us with, and it ministers to Him.

Many Old Testament scriptures exhorted Israel to "bless the Lord." This has become a religious cliché today. Now, people say "Bless the Lord" all the time, but the words themselves are not necessarily a blessing to God. Blessing the Lord is saying, "Father, I love You. Thank You that You are a good God. Thank You for moving in my life." Thanking God is what blesses Him.

The Effects of Praise

God has emotions. He isn't bound by His emotions the way that people are, but He has them. It ministers to God when you give Him praise. God gave everything for us. The least we can do is be thankful. In our own lives, we like to be thanked when we go out of our way to do something for somebody else. It's nice when someone acknowledges what we've done and says, "Thank you." Praise is simply a way of thanking God for all that He has done.

On one occasion, as Jesus was traveling from Galilee to Jerusalem, ten lepers called out to Him to have mercy on them (Luke 17:12-19). Jesus told them to go show themselves to the priest (the priest had to examine anyone who had been cured of leprosy to determine if they were clean). As they went on their way, they were cleansed. One of them, when he saw that he was healed, returned to Jesus and cried out in a loud voice giving thanks to God. Jesus replied,

> *Were there not ten cleansed? but where are the nine? There are not found that returned to give glory to God, save this stranger. And he said unto him, Arise, go thy way: thy faith hath made thee whole.*
>
> *Luke 17:17-19*

Leprosy is a disease that rots the skin and eventually causes digits and appendages to fall off. The Scripture says that ten were cleansed, but only the one who returned to thank God was made whole. I believe this is saying that the leprosy was stopped for all of them, but only one person was restored. Meaning, any part of his body that had fallen off was brought back. Restoration occurred because he came back to bless the Lord.

I remember taking my sons horseback riding one day when they were about six and four years old. It was a great day. We played in the creek, got dirty, ate junk food, and rode horses all day. At the end of the day, we got cleaned up and I put them to bed. As I was leaving my son Peter's room and turning out the light, he said, "Dad, you're a good dad!" Those words blessed me. It made me want to get him up out of bed and go do it all over again, just so I could hear him say it once more. Since that night, I've said to the Lord, "God, you're a good God," thousands of times.

I guarantee you that it blesses God when His children thank Him for how good He is. You were created for God's pleasure (Revelation 4:11), and blessing God makes Him want to bless you even more. In addition to building your faith to receive from the Lord and putting the devil to flight, praise ministers to God. It's a way for you to thank Him for what He has done in your life, and it will open up your heart to receive even more from Him.

Additional Resources:

1. *The Effects of Praise* is a three-part audio teaching available to listen to or download for free at http://www.awmi.net/extra/audio/1004

2. *The Effects of Praise* book by Andrew Wommack shows how the single act of praise begins to harvest peace, joy, pleasure, and contentment into every area of your life! Through praise, you can finally overcome anxiety, depression, and stress in your life. It is available through bookstores or the online store at http://www.awmi.net/store/usa/books/309

3. *How to Stay Positive in a Negative World* is a five-part audio teaching. If you watch the news, read the newspaper, or listen to the negative conversations of those around you long enough, and you'll find yourself discouraged. This teaching will show you how to how to rise above the noise of negativity and live your life according to the promises of God's Word. It is available to listen to or download for free at http://www.awmi.net/extra/audio/1065

"Ministering unto God" is an audio teaching available to listen to or download for free at http://www.awmi.net/extra/audio/k135

Chapter 12

Harnessing Your Emotions

L ife would be pretty boring without emotions. We'd just move from one bland experience to the next like a bunch of robots. Fortunately, God created us to experience life with emotions—but He never intended for us to be ruled and controlled by them. Out-of-control emotions make life miserable. As believers, we can't afford to let emotions run our lives.

I doubt there is a single person who loves God who wakes up in the morning saying, "I think I'll be depressed today" or "I want to be miserable." I can't imagine someone wanting to be under the control of damaging emotions. Yet when bad things start to happen, most people feel completely powerless to prevent negative emotions from dominating them. They don't realize that they have authority over their emotions, and it is within their power to harness them. The Word of God tells us,

> *Rejoice evermore. Pray without ceasing. In everything give thanks: for this is the will of God in Christ Jesus concerning you.*
>
> *1 Thessalonians 5:16-18*

This is just one of many scriptures that tell us to rejoice in all circumstances. God wouldn't have commanded us to control our emotions if we couldn't do it. The simple fact that we are commanded to rejoice and to praise God at all times is proof that we can.

God says we can harness our emotions, but popular culture encourages us to do the exact opposite. Psychologists tell people not to hold anything back. They say you have to vent, and let it all out. This viewpoint has its roots in the false assumption that our emotional state is an automatic response to the things that are happening to us in life. The idea is that you can't do anything to prevent emotion from rising up and controlling you, so you may as well let it all loose. But that isn't true. I don't deny that we can be hurt, or that we have negative emotional reactions to upsetting circumstances, but we can deny those emotions the opportunity to rule our lives.

I remember an instance when I was working with a ministry in Charlotte, North Carolina, feeding some homeless people. I was talking to an alcoholic and he got so mad that he spit a big glob of tobacco juice right in my face. Initially, I was mad. For a fraction of a second I wanted to punch his lights out, but I didn't. I knew that Jesus loved him, and I knew that I had love, joy, and peace abiding in my born-again spirit (Galatians 5:22). So, I denied anger the privilege of retaliating. I wiped the spit from my face and kept on preaching. I didn't miss a beat. I just kept telling him about how much God loved him, and I was able to operate from my born-again spirit rather than from my emotions.

The inability to harness your emotions when somebody spits in your face, hits you, insults you, ignores you, or stabs you in the back, will put you in bondage. You aren't free if emotions are dictating your behavior. The circumstances of your life are going to dominate you as long as you allow emotions to govern you.

Anyone who says that emotional responses to circumstances are inevitable, and that you can't stop those emotions from controlling you, has wrongly reduced human beings to merely evolved animals. You aren't a developed animal. You didn't evolve from fish or animals. You were created in the image of God, and you have a spirit man on the inside of you that gives you the capacity to operate above the animal level. You aren't reduced to just responding to stimuli from your environment. Your born-again spirit gives you the ability to live supernaturally. Listen to this:

> *Let no man say when he is tempted, I am tempted of God: for God cannot be tempted with evil, neither tempteth he any man: But every man is tempted, when he is drawn away of his own lust, and enticed. Then when lust hath conceived, it bringeth forth sin: and sin, when it is finished, bringeth forth death.*
>
> *James 1:13-15*

People today narrowly define "lust" as illicit sexual desire for another person, and while it is often used that way in scripture, it also means to long for, or desire. The meaning of "lust" in this scripture is "desire." Every man is tempted when he is lured away and enticed by his own desires, and then when desire (or emotion) conceives, it brings forth sin. Here's the point: Emotions aren't a byproduct of your environment. They are where sin is conceived.

The picture of sin being conceived and then giving birth to death is a mirror of the natural process of conception and childbirth. It's pretty simple: sexual relations lead to conception, and approximately forty weeks later, the woman gives birth. In the same way, once sin is conceived in your emotions, it will ultimately give birth to death. You can't see it right away, and it might take time, but sin will eventually give birth to death.

In the natural realm, if a man and a woman don't want to conceive a child, then they shouldn't have sexual relations. It works the same way in the spiritual realm. Every time you allow negative emotions to run amuck, you are conceiving sin. The problem is, most Christians don't recognize, or feel any responsibility for, that conception. People are letting their desires and emotions run wild, but then when the birth of sin and death starts to show, they don't want any part of it. Essentially, they have allowed the conception of sin in their emotions and now that they are nine months pregnant, they don't want to have a child. It doesn't work that way. You don't try to stop the birth—you stop conception. If there is a strong fight inside of you, pulling you toward sin, it's because you have already conceived the sin in your emotions. Stop the conception, and you won't have to worry about giving birth.

Sin doesn't come on you like the flu; it has to be conceived. You don't commit adultery accidentally; first, it has to be conceived in your emotions. It begins by allowing yourself to desire someone other than your spouse—that's the conception. It could be something as small as dreaming about the way some television character treats his or her spouse, and then beginning to indulge fantasies and live vicariously. People think there isn't anything wrong with that. They think since they aren't actually *doing* anything that there is no harm in it. They feel no accountability toward controlling their emotions.

I don't mean to be offensive, but in a spiritual sense, every time you indulge negative emotions it's like having spiritual intercourse with the devil. The devil is planting a seed on the inside of you that is going to grow into a sin, which eventually brings destruction. If you would recognize that, I guarantee it would change the way that you look at indulging emotions.

Instead of allowing depression and discouragement and other negative emotions to overrule you, recognize that the Bible tells us to be strong and of good courage in the face of trying circumstances (Joshua 1:9). The Word of God commands us in many places to harness our emotions. Every time you disobey those commands and allow yourself to slip into negative emotions, it's like having a spiritual affair with the devil. You know you shouldn't feel that way, but you feel like you can't help it so you give in. Giving up, or giving in, is going to plant a seed on the inside of you that will bring forth something you don't want. When the birth comes around, you're going to be crying out for God to save you.

You cannot afford to indulge your emotions and conceive sin if you want to live a victorious life. You have to learn to control your emotions.

The night Jesus was betrayed, He drew His disciples aside for some last instruction. The next day He would be crucified, and the disciples would be plunged into a terrible situation. Prior to the Resurrection, He knew that it would look like the devil had won. The crucifixion would make it appear like all of the faith and hope the disciples had put in Him was misplaced. Jesus was trying to build the disciples up to face that situation—to keep them from running away and being discouraged. The first words Jesus spoke during His last instructions to them were,

> *Let not your heart be troubled: ye believe in God, believe also in me.*
>
> *John 14:1*

"Let not your heart be troubled" is a command, not a suggestion. Jesus didn't say, "Try not to let your hearts be troubled." Our society, with its political correctness, would criticize Jesus for being so insensitive to the disciples as to suggest they shouldn't be troubled during a devastating time. Our culture would advise the disciples to let it all out and vent their emotions. Jesus did just the opposite.

I believe it is significant that the very first thing Jesus told His disciples to do was to harness their emotions. In my experience with myself and in dealing with others in crisis, I have found that reaction to the initial moments of a crisis is vital. If you fall apart like a two-dollar suitcase at the very beginning—if you let fear, despair, grief, and sorrow overwhelm you—it's nearly impossible to overcome those emotions and walk in faith later on. It's a lot easier to stop those emotions from ever entering in than it is to try to keep them from getting out after you have been entertaining them.

My oldest son Joshua called me one night and said, "Dad, I'm sorry to tell you this but Peter (my younger son) is dead." Joshua told me what had happened and explained that they were at the hospital. Peter had been dead about four hours by the time Joshua called. I said, "The first report is not the last report. Don't let anybody touch him until we get there."

Harnessing Your Emotions

My wife, Jamie, and I got into our car and began the hour drive to the hospital. I started to have the same emotions that any parent would have in a similar situation. I began feeling grief, sorrow, confusion, and fear. All kinds of emotions were swirling around in me. But I remembered this teaching, that Jesus commanded His disciples to not let their hearts be troubled as they were entering into a crisis situation. So, I refused to give in to those negative emotions.

As we were driving toward the hospital, I started giving thanks to God and worshipping Him. I said, "God, I know You didn't kill my son. You are not the one who caused this problem, and whether he comes back to life or not, I want You to know that I am going to continue to serve You. You are a good God." I believe with all of my heart that praising God was the key to not letting my emotions run away. I kept them under control. I began to operate in faith and joy instead of grief and sorrow.

I'm not condemning anyone who has experienced sorrow and grief in a crisis. I understand that we are human and that we have these emotions. I also know that experiences in life can knock the wind out of you. I'm just saying that we aren't only human. You *can* operate above your emotions when tragedy strikes, if you choose to.

When Jamie and I got into town, we found out that Peter had come back to life. After nearly five hours of being dead, Peter suddenly sat up and started talking. There was no brain damage of any kind. Today he's not only alive and well, but we have a granddaughter who was born a year later. I honestly believe that none of this would have happened if I had let my emotions run away with me. Jesus gave us a command to control our emotions

117

in a crisis because giving in to fear prevents us from trusting in God, and it blocks us from receiving from God by faith. Venting or indulging negative emotions only makes them grow, like adding fuel to a fire—making it more and more difficult to walk in faith.

Over the years, I've had several horses, and I can tell you that if you let a horse run away with you, it is nearly impossible to rein it in. It is very difficult to overcome a horse's runaway momentum. On the other hand, I've taught a seven-year-old boy how to control a relatively wild horse by following a few simple instructions. He rode my horse for nearly two hours without any problems. Shortly after the seven year old dismounted my horse, a twenty-year-old young man showed up at my place wanting to ride. By contrast, the young man didn't want to listen to any of my instructions. Within minutes, the horse took off running and he couldn't stop it. Eventually, the horse threw the young man off, and he ended up making a trip to the hospital.

Emotions are like horses: it's a lot easier to keep them in check than it is to rein them in after they have begun to run wild. If you fall to pieces the moment something bad happens, it's going to be a lot harder to pull yourself back together and start believing God for a miracle. It's much easier to harness your emotions from the start. Thankfully, God has given you the power to do so.

You can rule over your emotions. You don't have to let them lead you around by the nose. Part of growing up is learning not to be controlled by your emotions. When you're a kid, all you want to do is go play and have fun. As you mature, you learn to work even when you don't want to. You may not feel like being the parent or going to work on a given day, but you do it anyway because it's part of being a responsible adult. Being mature means doing things even when we don't feel like it. Being a mature believer means the same thing. You can choose not to let negative emotions run wild and dominate you.

God has not only given us the authority to rule and reign over our emotions, He has also commanded us to use that authority. Jesus said,

> *In the world ye shall have tribulation: but be of good cheer; I have overcome the world.*
>
> *John 16:33*

The Lord is saying that you are going to have problems in this life, but He says, "be of good cheer." He's not saying we should only rejoice when everything is perfect in life. This is a command to be of good cheer regardless of our problems. God wouldn't command us to rejoice if we weren't capable of doing it.

Harnessing your emotions is an essential component to living a victorious Christian life—not just in a crisis situation, but in everyday life. When bad news comes, don't give in to the temptation to let negative emotions like fear and depression rush in and take control of you. Instead, make the choice to rejoice in the Lord and remember that you have God's love, joy, and peace abiding in your born-again spirit. Even when life is going great, you still need to harness your emotions because that is where sin is conceived. Avoid the conception in your emotions, and you won't find yourself in a fight to avoid giving birth to sin.

Sharper than a Two-Edged Sword

Additional Resources:

1.*Harnessing Your Emotions* is a four-part audio teaching available to listen to or download for free at http://www.awmi.net/extra/audio/1005

2.*Harnessing Your Emotions* book by Andrew Wommack will give you a look at who you are in Christ that very few Christians have seen. This is life-changing information, and one of the major keys to a victorious life in Christ. It is available through bookstores or the online store at http://www.awmi.net/store/usa/books/313

3.*Anger Management* is a four-part audio teaching, in which Andrew shares truths from God's Word on the subject of anger that are as rare as gold. It is available to listen to or download for free at http://www.awmi.net/extra/audio/1044

God's Kind of Love through You is a nine-part audio teaching. Once you understand how much God loves you, it will compel you to allow God's love to flow through you. However, there are many misunderstandings about what that means and how to do it. This series will help. It is available to listen to or download for free at http://www.awmi.net/extra/audio/1055

120

Chapter 13

Discover the Keys to Staying Full of God

"We're like a bucket full of holes," I've heard people say. "Even though God fills us up with His power, it just leaks out again, and we have to be constantly refilled." Well, that might be an accurate description of many people's life experience, but I don't believe that God designed us to be leaky vessels. I don't think that encounters with God come with an expiration date, and then you need to go get a new dose of the Holy Spirit. My personal experience is completely contrary to that. God has done things in my life that have never gotten old. They just keep getting better.

The importance of staying full of the love of God was brought home to me one day after speaking at a small church in Louisville, Kentucky. A woman approached me on Sunday morning to tell me how she had been affected by the services I held that week. She was crying as she told me how full of God she was, and how experiencing the love of God had changed her life. Then she qualified it all by saying, "I know that in a month or so I'll lose it and go back to the way I was, but right now I feel awesome."

It grieved me to hear this woman anticipate losing the joy of the Lord that she had discovered. I was speaking at the church again that night, so I went back to my hotel and began praying specifically for her. I didn't believe the impact of her experience with God needed to fade away. As I prayed, I began thinking about my own experiences with God.

The Lord miraculously revealed himself to me on March 23, 1968. Here I am, decades later, and that experience has not worn off. As a matter of fact, it's more real to me today than it was in 1968. I was emotionally touched the night it happened, but today I have a depth of understanding that I didn't have back then. What God did that night has soaked down into every part of my being. I haven't lost the power of that encounter; it has become stronger.

As I sat in my hotel room remembering what God had done in me, it reinforced my belief that we don't have to leak out the love of God like a broken vessel. "God," I was praying, "I know it doesn't have to be this way. We don't have to lose the revelation of how much You love us. What can I tell this woman? How can I help her?" I was asking God for revelation, and He directed me to the following scripture:

> *Because that, when they knew God, they glorified him not as God, neither were thankful; but became vain in their imaginations, and their foolish heart was darkened.*
>
> *Romans 1:21*

Leading up to this verse, the Apostle Paul had been explaining in his letter to the Romans that although everyone has an intuitive knowledge of God, it is possible to dull yourself to that knowledge of Him. Beginning with this verse, Paul began to describe the progressive steps that people take to desensitize themselves to the Lord—steps that have the effect of decreasing the impact God has on their lives.

The Lord spoke to me through this to show that there is a reason people feel like leaky vessels. There is a reason the things God does in someone's life don't seem to last, but it has nothing to do with God withdrawing His presence. It isn't because there is an expiration date on the power He releases in our lives. Our own actions are what decrease the effectiveness of God's touch in our lives. It's what we do, not what God does.

This passage of scripture describes four progressive steps that people take to harden their hearts toward God. We can discover the keys to staying full of God simply by turning those steps around and doing the opposite.

The Scripture says that, "when they knew God, they glorified him not as God." To glorify means to render or esteem glorious. Another way of saying it is "to value," or "to prize." So, this verse is saying that the first step in hardening your heart is to stop valuing or prizing God. The reason people lose the power of what God has done in their lives is because they stop placing the proper value on it. They don't esteem what God has done, and eventually it loses its effectiveness in their lives.

If you had something that you really valued, you probably wouldn't leave it laying on the front seat of an unlocked car while you went into the store; it might get stolen. You'd take precautions— like hiding it under the seat or leaving someone in the car to guard it. On the other hand, you wouldn't worry too much about a penny laying on the floorboard. The penny will sit neglected upon the floor mat until it is eventually lost or sucked up by a vacuum hose. When you value something, you treat it differently. The sad thing is that most people don't value what God has done in their lives.

Neglecting God is what causes people to feel like a leaky vessel.

Misplaced values diminish the impact God has in our lives. Most people place a higher value on circumstances or the opinions of others than they do on God. Your attention works like a magnifying glass: whatever you focus on gets bigger, and whatever you neglect diminishes. If you focus on the Word of God, then the Lord will take on greater importance in your life. Whereas focusing on the opinions of others will cause your understanding of God's view of you to shrink by comparison. It's like a seesaw, or a pair of scales: both ends can't be up at the same time. You can't truly value what God is saying about you and value what other people are saying at the same time.

I stood up in church the morning after my encounter with God back in 1968 and told everyone that I was filled with the Holy Spirit and the love of God. I didn't know what had happened to me. I was just trying to explain it the best I could. The pastor came up to me afterward to reprimand me for saying I was filled with the Spirit. "Peter was filled with the Holy Spirit," he said, "and Paul was filled with the Holy Spirit, but people aren't filled with the Spirit today. You're trying to make yourself out to be superior to the rest of us." For the first time in my life I understood that God loved me, and immediately someone came along to try to devalue what God had done.

Not long after, I felt like God was telling me to quit college. It was the height of the Vietnam War and quitting school meant I would be drafted, so my mother sent everyone she knew to tell me what a bad idea it was. There was a tendency for me to value what they were saying, because I respected all of those people. But by the grace of God, I stayed steady and focused on what the Lord was doing in my life.

I quit school a little while later, and sure enough I was reclassified for the draft. A military recruiter came to my house to talk about my options. He sat down, opened up his briefcase, spread out all of his promotional materials, and began to tell me the advantages of enlisting in the Army of my own accord rather than waiting to be drafted.

The recruiter started his sales pitch and I said, "I can save us both a lot of time."

"Really," he answered, "how's that?"

"It's possible I'll get drafted because I quit school and lost my student deferment, right?" I asked.

"That's right," he said.

"But you don't understand," I said, "God told me to quit school, so I'm doing what God told me to do. If God wants me to get drafted, I will be. But if He doesn't, I won't be."

The recruiter burst into laughter. "Boy," he said, "I can guarantee you, you are going to Vietnam!"

I was valuing God and what God had spoken to me, but the recruiter didn't value God at all. In his mind, he was a representative of the United States government—the most powerful force on earth. He wanted me to esteem his opinion higher than I esteemed God's. The recruiter's total disregard for God made me angry.

I leaned over and started poking my finger in his chest as I said, "Buddy, if God wants me drafted, then I'll be drafted. But if He doesn't, you or the United States government or every demon in hell can't draft me!"

The recruiter quietly gathered all of his brochures, stood up, and walked out the front door without saying another word.

I found my draft notice in the mailbox the very next morning. I'm not even sure it was mailed. I wish I had bothered to check to see if there was a stamp or postmark on the envelope. I wouldn't be surprised if that recruiter went back to his office and processed my draft paperwork himself, and then stuck it in my mailbox. But I didn't care. I was glorifying God.

Each of those situations was an opportunity for me to shift my focus away from God and toward the opinions of other people. If I had valued their opinions above God's, I would have taken the first step toward losing the joy of knowing that God loved me. I didn't know a lot back then, but by the grace of God I esteemed Him greater than anything else. As a result, I stayed full of the love and joy of the Lord.

I've been through some terrible situations that could have drawn my focus away from God. I've been kidnapped, threatened, and insulted. I've had people burn my books in protest. I've had all sorts of bad things happen to me, but—glory to God—I've never esteemed other people's opinions more than what God has said to me. This has been a key factor in helping me stay full of God's love over the years. You have to keep putting value on what God has said and done in your life.

One day as I was hiking up Pikes Peak with a friend, he began telling me some things that another friend of ours was saying about us behind our backs. It doesn't bless me to hear other people criticizing me, but I also don't focus on it because to do so would diminish the value I place on what God has said about me. So, I said to him, "Look, I don't want to hear it. I know what he thinks of me, and I just don't want to hear it anymore."

My friend was quiet for a while, and then he said, "Why doesn't what he is saying bother you, like it bothers me?"

"Because I don't value his opinion as much as you do," I answered.

The things that other people say will only really upset you if you esteem their opinion. I'm not saying you shouldn't value what anybody else says—especially if you live with them—but in comparison with the value you place on God's Word, nobody else's opinion should matter.

But glorifying God and magnifying Him above your circumstances is only the first key to staying full of God. After mentioning that the people failed to glorify God, the Scripture says: "neither were [they] thankful; but became vain in their imaginations, and their foolish heart was darkened" (Romans 1:21). The other keys to staying full of God are being thankful, having a godly imagination, and guarding your heart.

Bless the LORD, O my soul: and all that is within me, bless his holy name. Bless the LORD, O my soul, and forget not all his benefits.

Psalm 103:1-2

Thankfulness is closely related to glorifying God. In fact, you can't really do one without the other. Being thankful involves remembering what God has done for you and offering Him praise in return. It is an attitude of glorifying God, magnifying Him above all else, and expressing gratitude for His goodness. Christians ought to be the most thankful people on the face of the planet, because we have the most to be grateful for.

Imagination is often thought of as something for kids, and adults overlook its importance, but imagination is where you conceive the things of God. Imagination is forming a mental picture of something that isn't real to the senses. We think with pictures. It's how we do anything from giving directions to solving problems, and having a godly imagination is essential to staying full of God. For instance, you aren't likely to see healing manifest in your body if you imagine yourself to be a sick person. If you see yourself sick, that's what you will be. As a man thinks in his heart, so is he (Proverbs 23:7), so you want your imagination working for you—not against you. In Scripture, hope is the word that is used for a positive imagination that is working in your favor.

The final key to staying full of God is a good heart. The heart is what we live from. It is the ground from which our life grows.

Jesus said,

A good man out of the good treasure of the heart bringeth forth good things: and an evil man out of the evil treasure bringeth forth evil things.

Matthew 12:35

Your behavior and words spring forth from your heart, so staying full of God means having a heart that is filled with the Word of God. You can only imagine yourself as God sees you and you can only live that image out, if the Word of God has established in your heart who God says you are. The Word of God is the seed you must plant in your heart if you want to see God's love grow and bear fruit in your life.

I have barely scratched the surface of what it means to stay full of God, but these are the key issues: prize Him above all else, maintain an attitude of thankfulness for His goodness, conceive the things of God in your imagination, and make sure you are filling your heart with godly treasure.

You don't have to leak the love that God is pouring into you, or the blessings He is pouring into your life. The four principles discussed here describe a lifestyle of focusing on the Lord, and they will give you an eternal perspective that will keep you full of God—even during times of trouble.

Additional Resources:

1.*Discover the Keys to Staying Full of God* is a four-part audio teaching available to listen to or download for free at http://www.awmi.net/extra/audio/1029

2.*Discover the Keys to Staying Full of God* book by Andrew Wommack reveals the essentials to a strong, close relationship with God. It is available through bookstores or the online store at http://www.awmi.net/store/usa/books/324

Don't Limit God is a five-part audio teaching. Most Christians believe that God, in His sovereignty, does what He wants on earth. Is that true, or is it possible that He has limited Himself by His own words? If He has, then may be the only limits in your life have been placed there by you. Combine this understanding with "Staying Full of God," and watch the limits in your life fade away. It is available to listen to or download for free at http://www.awmi.net/extra/audio/1060

Chapter 14

God Wants You Well

Nearly everyone recognizes that God has the power to heal, but not many people have confidence that God wants to heal *them*. God is concerned about more than your emotional well-being. He wants your physical body to be healthy also. Sadly, some people are teaching that God controls everything in this world, and that no one can get sick unless God wills it—but that is absolutely wrong. God doesn't give people cancer. It isn't God's will for children to be sick or for anyone to be born with a disability. God wants His children to be well, and Jesus paid the price to purchase health for us.

Healing doesn't happen accidentally. In our fallen world, it's easier to get sick than it is to be well. Everything in the natural world goes from good to bad, and from health to sickness. If you want to receive healing, you have to pursue it. You can't just throw a prayer out there, half hoping that God might do something. You won't get healed by saying, "God I know You can heal, and *if* it be Your will then heal me." You have to *know* it is God's will to heal when you pray. In my estimation, grabbing hold of the truth that God wants you well is one of the most important steps you can take toward receiving healing.

It is popular in some circles to think that God causes sickness, or allows it, in order to accomplish His will or to teach you something. Nothing could be further from the truth. For one thing, if you believe it is God's will for you to be sick, then you shouldn't fight against Him by going to the doctor and trying to get better. I don't think anyone would argue that it is wrong to want to be healthy. Even the people who think God is the source of illness believe it is okay to try to get better. Yet if it is God's will for you to be sick, then you shouldn't try to get well; you should stay sick and learn what God is trying to teach you. But it isn't God's will for you to be sick, and He never causes your sickness to teach you anything.

We should be fighting against sickness. God has clearly revealed that His will is for us to be well, not sick. And we aren't merely hoping that God wants us well, we know it. Scripture says,

> *Who being the brightness of his glory, and the express image of his person, and upholding all things by the word of his power, when he had by himself purged our sins, sat down on the right hand of the Majesty on high.*
>
> *Hebrews 1:3*

Jesus is the brightness of God's glory and the express image of His person. This scripture isn't talking about an "image" that hints at the glory of God the Father. No, the Greek used here means a perfect representation. Jesus is the perfect representation of God the Father. Jesus said that He only did what He saw His Father do, and He told His disciples that to see Him was to see the Father (John 14:9). Jesus represented God perfectly, so if we want to know God's will concerning healing, all we have to do is examine the life and teachings of Jesus.

Jesus never caused anyone to be sick, and He didn't use sickness to teach people lessons. Yet people today are saying God has "blessed" them with sickness because it captured their attention and drew them to the Lord. People are crediting God with making them paralyzed or ill, but Jesus never used illness to accomplish His will. Sickness is never a "blessing in disguise," it's a curse (Deuteronomy 28:15-68).

There is not a single example in Scripture of Jesus doing the things that religion is blaming God for today. Jesus said, "...he that hath seen me hath seen the Father." One of the greatest testimonies in Scripture that God wants you well is the fact that Jesus' life expressly shows His desire to heal the sick.

When the Apostle Peter was preaching the Gospel to the Gentile household of Cornelius, he summarized the life and ministry of Jesus by saying:

> *How God anointed Jesus of Nazareth with the Holy Ghost and with power: who went about doing good, and healing all that were oppressed of the devil; for God was with him.*
>
> *Acts 10:38*

It says that Jesus "went about doing good." Not only did Jesus heal those who were oppressed of the devil, He healed them *all*. He didn't just go around healing some people. Jesus' actions are a demonstration of God's will to heal everyone, not just a select few.

Teaching that God uses sickness to accomplish His will causes people to drop their guard and to embrace something that is actually from the devil. Scripture says that those whom Jesus healed were oppressed by the devil, not by God. The Lord's command to us is clear:

> *Submit yourselves therefore to God. Resist the devil, and he will flee from you.*
>
> *James 4:7*

Some things in life are from God. Other things are from the devil. We are supposed to submit to God, and resist the devil. Anyone who wrongly interprets sickness as being from God is submitting to the devil instead of resisting him. It is important to know when to submit and when to resist.

Religion is the source of a lot of confusion. It replaces a vibrant relationship with God through Jesus, with obeying rules and regulations. In the case of healing, religion teaches that sickness is a blessing in disguise, and that God uses it to humble you or to make you a better person. It is calling evil good, and good evil. In effect, this confusion causes you to embrace the devil and prevents you from receiving healing from God. Obviously, sickness is not going to flee from you as long as you are embracing it. You have to resist the devil in order to make him flee.

To effectively resist the devil, you have to understand that God wants you well when you pray, because half-efforts at resistance won't work. The Bible says,

> *If any of you lack wisdom, let him ask of God, that giveth to all men liberally, and upbraideth not; and it shall be given him. But let him ask in faith, nothing wavering. For he that wavereth is like a wave of the sea driven with the wind and tossed. For*

let not that man think that he shall receive any thing of the Lord. A double minded man is unstable in all his ways.

James 1:5-8

This principle of not wavering when you petition God isn't limited to requesting wisdom. It can be applied to healing also: you won't receive healing if you are asking God to heal you, but at the same time wavering in your heart about whether or not it is God's will to heal. That's being double minded, and you won't receive anything that way. You have to believe you receive when you pray (Mark 11:24). In order to believe without wavering when you pray, you have to know that God wants you well. It must be settled in your heart.

God is not the author of sickness, and He doesn't use sickness—or any other kind of evil—to accomplish His will. God has nothing whatsoever to do with sickness. James, a leader in the early Jerusalem church, wrote:

> *Let no man say when he is tempted, I am tempted of God: for God cannot be tempted with evil, neither tempteth he any man...Every good gift and every perfect gift is from above, and cometh down from the Father of lights, with whom is no variableness, neither shadow of turning.*
>
> *James 1:13 and 17*

Wrongly believing that God is behind sickness, pain, and suffering is going to affect your understanding of His love. Associating God with sickness is propaganda from the enemy. The idea behind propaganda is that if you repeat the lie enough times, people will start believing it. Even if you can see the fallacy, the lie can work its way into your belief system because you start thinking that there must be some truth to something you hear over and over again. Religion mentions that God loves us, but then goes on to say that God makes babies sick, or gives people cancer because He loves them and wants to teach them something. That isn't love.

Imagine if a man had the power to give you cancer, cause debilitating pain, or inflict babies with deformities. After he had done those things, no one would look to him and suppose he did it out of love. There isn't a civilized nation on the face of the earth that wouldn't prosecute him to the fullest extent of the law. A man such as that would be thrown in prison for criminal behavior. Yet religion is trying to say that God causes tragedy because He loves you. It is a lie that has been repeated so often, people have started believing it.

The destructive power of this lie is that it renders you unable to reconcile the love of God with the use of sickness as a teaching tool. Deep down in your heart, whether you understand it or not, it's going to affect your relationship with God and your understanding of how much He loves you. You can't blame God for causing tragedy in your life and trust Him wholeheartedly at the same time.

I read a news article about the recent earthquakes in Haiti that was exploring questions surrounding the tragedy, and how such a terrible thing could happen. Several people were quoted as saying that the earthquake was God's judgment upon the nation for its history of voodoo or other problems in society. The author was describing how so much blame for the tragedy was being placed on God that it was shaking the faith of many Haitians.

The article contained a poignant photograph. Dozens and dozens of corpses could be seen piled high in a mound, testifying to the immense cost of life, and the mound itself was being consumed by flames as part of a drastic effort to stop the spread of disease. In front of the fire, an elderly woman was frozen in time as she walked by. She must have reached into her purse and pulled out her Bible just before the photo was taken. Although her arm was captured in stillness, the action was clear: she was tossing her Bible onto the heap of burning bodies. It's not surprising to see people reject God when they are told He is responsible for the death and pain in their life.

Jesus "went about doing good." It is good to be well—it's bad to be sick. Sickness is not a blessing from God sent to make you holy. Sickness is an attack from the devil. Sometimes it is completely demonic and spiritual in its origin, other times it is just the result of living in a fallen world, but sickness and tragedy are never from God. Jesus, out of His great love, took our sin *and* our sicknesses upon His body on the cross. The Word of God is very clear on this point:

> *Surely he hath borne our griefs, and carried our sorrows: yet*
> *we did esteem him stricken, smitten of God, and afflicted. But*
> *he was wounded for our transgressions, he was bruised for our*
> *iniquities: the chastisement of our peace was upon him; and*
> *with his stripes we are healed.*
>
> *Isaiah 53:4-5*

This bold declaration clearly says that by the stripes of Jesus we are healed. Religion enters in with its customary confusion and tries to spiritualize this scripture by saying we are only healed in our hearts. Religion says this means that in your heart and emotions you were healed from the hurt and the pain of sin. It is true to say that, but it isn't the whole truth. Yes, Jesus came to set us free emotionally and spiritually, but He didn't stop there. This scripture also applies to the healing of our physical bodies. The Gospel of Matthew tells how the people brought their sick to Jesus and He healed them *all* (showing His desire to heal everyone), and then it references this exact prophecy, saying,

> *That it might be fulfilled which was spoken by Esaias the prophet, saying, Himself took our infirmities, and bare our sicknesses.*
>
> *Matthew 8:17*

Jesus took our infirmities and bore our sicknesses in His body on the cross. It is a part of the atonement of the Lord Jesus Christ for you to be healed. Jesus doesn't want you to be sick any more than He wants you to sin.

Again, religion will try to confuse the matter by pointing out that Christians die of sickness—even some who believed God would heal them. Religion concludes that it must not have been God's will to heal in those cases, rather than accepting the possibility that healing was available but, for some reason, those people weren't able to reach out and take advantage of God's healing power. Rather than risk hurting anyone's feelings or accepting any responsibility, religion places the blame on God.

I don't know why everyone who believes for healing isn't healed, but I know it isn't God's fault. Whatever unanswered questions we have about healing do not change the fact that the express will of

God, as seen in the life of Jesus and written in the Word, is that God wants you well. Jesus paid for sickness in the atonement so that you can be well, and untold numbers of people are being healed by the power of God all over the world today.

The Bible puts the healing of your physical body and forgiveness of your sins in the same category. It's a package deal. They even appear together in the same verses:

> *Bless the LORD, O my soul, and forget not all his benefits: Who forgiveth all thine iniquities; who healeth all thy diseases.*
>
> *Psalm 103:2-3*

> *Who his own self bare our sins in his own body on the tree, that we, being dead to sins, should live unto righteousness: by whose stripes ye were healed.*
>
> *1 Peter 2:24*

There is simply no doubt that Jesus provided for healing in the atonement and that God wants you well. In fact, the Greek word *sozo* that is translated "save" over 300 times in the New Testament is also used to describe healing. It means to save, make whole, or to heal. A classic example of the use of this word *sozo* is found in the letter of James:

> *Is any sick among you? let him call for the elders of the church; and let them pray over him, anointing him with oil in the name of the Lord: And the prayer of faith shall save the sick, and the Lord shall raise him up; and if he have committed sins, they shall be forgiven him.*
>
> *James 5:14-15*

It's obvious that the physical body is what will be healed. Some in our time have tried to separate salvation and healing by saying that salvation is for everyone, but healing is an add-on, like it costs extra. That just isn't true. The Bible unquestionably teaches that Jesus died to heal your body at the same time He died to forgive your sins. You are just as much healed by the stripes of Jesus as you are forgiven and made righteous by His sacrifice.

Jesus would no more put sickness on you than He would lead you into sin. He wants you well just as much as He wants you forgiven of your sins. The first step in receiving healing is to know beyond a doubt that God wants you well. You have to understand that God is not only capable of healing, but He wants to heal you. Once you understand that, it will be easy to believe in your heart when you pray for healing, and to see yourself healed.

Additional Resources:

1.*Healing Testimonies* are six different videos documenting healings that have occurred through some contact with Andrew Wommack Ministries. See the evidence of God working miracles. These stories will encourage you and build your faith. They are available to view free at http://www.awmi.net/extra/healing

2.*Healing Journeys* volumes one and two are available for purchase through the online store at http://www.awmi.net/store/usa/videos Each DVD documents five different stories of the power of God's Word working in the lives of people.

3.*God Wants You Well* is a book by Andrew Wommack. In this book, Andrew shares the truth of what God's unconditional love and grace has already provided. Healing is a big part of that provision. He answers many common questions including those about Paul's thorn in the flesh, the sovereignty of God and more. If you or someone you know is in need of healing, this book is for you. It is available through bookstores or the online store at http://www.awmi.net/store/usa/books/330

4.*God Wants You Well* is a four-part audio teaching available to listen to or download for free at http://www.awmi.net/extra/audio/1036

5."Healing Scriptures" is a collection of healing scriptures with soft background music. As you listen, your mind will be able to relax, and your faith will be built to receive your healing. It is available to listen to or download for free at http://www.awmi.net/extra/audio/i05

6.*How To Receive a Miracle* is a three-part audio teaching that will show you how to grab a hold of miracles and make them happen. It is available to listen to or download for free at http://www.awmi.net/extra/audio/1006

The Good Report: God Wants You Well booklet by Andrew Wommack is a compilation of articles on the topic of healing. It is available through the online store at   http://www.awmi.net/store/usa/books/102

Sharper than a Two-Edged Sword

Chapter 15

Hardness of Heart

We all have a heart condition. I'm not talking about your physical heart, but about your affections and attentions. The condition of your heart determines how much the Holy Spirit can penetrate. A hardened heart is cold, insensitive, unfeeling, and unyielding. It can either be hardened toward the world or toward God. The Lord made us in such a way that whatever we focus our hearts upon—whatever we delight in—we become sensitive to, and whatever we neglect, we become hardened to. Someone who is more comfortable with the natural realm than with the spiritual realm has a heart that is hardened toward God. Thankfully, you can become sensitive to God and hardened to the world. You simply have to change what you delight in, or what you focus your attentions and affections on.

Our level of sensitivity to God varies in different areas. You may be very sensitive to God in one area, but hardened in another. In my own case, I latched on to healing when I was young, and I was very sensitive to God in that area. I saw great miracles of healing happen, yet I struggled with prosperity for a long time. I was receptive to God in the area of healing, but hardened in the sphere of prosperity. It took years for me to get the same level of sensitivity toward prosperity that I had toward healing.

A hardened heart will cause you to not perceive things that should be obvious. Right after Jesus fed 5,000 people with five small loaves of bread and two fish, He put His disciples in a boat and sent them across the Sea of Galilee. Then Jesus sent the crowd away and went up on a mountain to pray. During the night, a storm rose up on the sea and Jesus could see the disciples struggling in their boat against the wind and the waves. Jesus walked across the water, climbed into the boat, and commanded the storm to be still. The disciples' response is recorded in Scripture:

> *They were sore amazed in themselves beyond measure, and wondered. For they considered not the miracle of the loaves: for their heart was hardened.*
>
> *Mark 6:51-52*

The disciples had just watched Jesus feed thousands of people using five loaves of bread and two small fish. They should not have been shocked to see Him perform another great miracle, but they were. They were amazed beyond measure to see Jesus walk on water because their hearts were hardened. If we can become more sensitive to God than to the world, it won't surprise us to see Jesus come walking on top of the problem that is about to drown us. We can get to a place where the supernatural becomes normal. First, we need to understand what it is that hardens our hearts toward God so we can reverse the process.

Mark 6:52 says the disciples hearts were hardened because they didn't consider the miracle of the feeding of the five thousand. The word *consider* means, "to study, ponder, deliberate, examine" or the scriptural word would be to meditate. Whatever we focus on, our hearts become sensitive to and whatever we neglect, our hearts become hardened to. These disciples weren't focused on sin, they were focused on trying to stay alive in the midst of a storm. But it took their attention away from the miracle they had just witnessed and hardened their hearts towards God.

The disciples continued to have trouble perceiving spiritual reality. After many more miracles, Jesus commented on their hardness of heart:

> *And when Jesus knew it, he saith unto them, Why reason ye, because ye have no bread?   perceive ye not yet, neither understand? have ye your heart yet hardened? Having eyes, see ye not? and having ears, hear ye not? and do ye not remember?*
>
> *Mark 8:17-18*

The inability to perceive is characteristic of a hardened heart. When you have a hardened heart, you see with your physical eyes, but you can't see with your heart. You have physical ears, but you can't hear the voice of God in your heart, and you can't remember spiritual things. Anyone who is having trouble perceiving, understanding, or remembering the things of God has a hardened heart. In simple terms, a hardened heart causes spiritual dullness. It prevents you from functioning the way that God intends, and it keeps you from perceiving spiritual truths.

Hardening of the heart in one area is a byproduct of what you focus your attention on. Your heart becomes sensitive to what you consider, and it becomes hardened toward the things you aren't meditating on. Either you focus your attention on God and become numb to the things of the world, or you focus on the cares of this world and become inattentive to God. In both cases, the heart is gradually hardened toward what you neglect and sensitized to whatever you set your affections on.

Jesus described this process as "waxing gross" (Matthew 13:15). This term is descriptive of the method used to make candles. A wick was repeatedly dipped in melted wax and lifted out. Each time it was lifted out, a layer of wax would harden around the wick. This would be done hundreds of times until enough wax built up to form a candle. Similarly, a heart waxes gross by repeatedly neglecting God. It doesn't become hard in a moment. Layer after layer of neglect builds up insensitivity as we focus our attention on something other than God.

I have loved God and sought Him my entire life, but there were times when I allowed other things to occupy my attention. That neglect hardened me toward God to a degree. I had knowledge of the truths of the kingdom of God, but they weren't working for me the way that they should have been. Specifically, I knew it was God's will to heal, but I wasn't seeing many people get healed. I believed in healing, and I could quote scriptures to you, but I wasn't giving priority to the Word of God in my life. I was letting other things occupy me. As a result, my heart hardened toward God and I wasn't experiencing the full impact of God's will to heal.

In the book of Hebrews, the author detailed some noteworthy acts of faith that are recorded in the Word of God. While discussing the faith of Abraham and Sarah, the author wrote:

Hardness of Heart

And truly, if they had been mindful of that country from whence they came out, they might have had opportunity to have returned.

Hebrews 11:15

This verse may not be one that is highlighted in your Bible, but it contains a profound truth. God called Abraham and Sarah to leave the land they were from and go into a land that He would show them later. In other words, God told them to leave, but He didn't tell them where they were going. They left their home in faith and journeyed out into the unknown. This scripture says that if their minds had been full of, or focused on, what they left behind, they might have had opportunity to return to it. The Lord never intended for them to go back, so any "opportunity" to return would have been a temptation. Abraham and Sarah weren't mindful of the country they came out of, so they weren't even tempted to return.

This reveals the positive side of hardening your heart: like Abraham and Sarah, you can harden your heart toward the world and temptation. **The simple truth is that you can't be tempted by what you don't think about.** As you neglect doubt and unbelief, your heart will begin to become insensitive to those things. Eventually, you can become hardened toward sin and failure.

In the world, we see the opposite of this happening. People are focusing on the world, and they have become sensitive to sin. For instance, I have people come to me all the time who want to be set free from struggles with sexual lust. Inevitably, as I talk to them, they reveal that they are focused on sex. Many times they are into pornography, or they are exposing themselves to sexual content

147

on the Internet or in R-rated movies. Even if you are watching Christian programs on television, the commercials will kill you. Sex is used to sell everything. Popular culture is bombarding society with sexual immorality. You cannot watch that stuff and not be tempted with lustful thoughts. Stop thinking about it, stop watching it, stop focusing your attention on it, and you won't be tempted.

We live in the world, but we don't have to be part of it (John 17:14). I'm not suggesting that we all move into monasteries or bury our heads in the sand. We are the salt of the earth, and to do any good we have to get out of the saltshaker. The Lord doesn't want us to retreat from the world. On the contrary, we need to let our light illuminate the world. But I can also guarantee you that God doesn't want us to be plugged into the world, taking in the same garbage as unbelievers.

The average Christian today is watching the same television shows, reading the same books, and going to the same movies as the average unbeliever—and they are getting the exact same results. They are just as broke and sick as their unbelieving neighbors. If you put nothing but garbage into your heart, you'll get nothing but garbage back out into your life.

The modern lifestyle of exposure to sin and carnality will harden your heart. It puts a layer of insensitivity between you and God. If you want your heart to be really sensitive to God, then you have to reverse this process. You have to spend more time seeking God than you do plugging in to the junk that this world has to offer. It's that simple.

A lot of people understand that God has better plans for their lives than they are experiencing. They know God wants them well, prospering, and living an abundant life. They have studied the Word, they go to church, and they know that there is an abundant life out there waiting for them. Most people can see those blessings, but very few people have sought God to the degree that their heart is sensitive enough to receive those benefits.

God isn't withholding His blessings from you until you try hard enough. Your heart just isn't capable of receiving God's blessings when it is hardened toward Him. The solution is to focus your attention on God, and harden your heart to the world.

I was born again when I was eight years old, but when I was eighteen, I had an encounter with God that changed my life. I experienced His love for me, and after that I became a stark-raving-mad fanatic in love with God. My mother thought I had gone a little too far, and she signed me up for a trip to Europe with a group of Baptist kids in the hope that it would bring me back to earth. I guess she thought it would give me a different perspective on life. Having been raised in Arlington, Texas, I was never exposed to a lot of the things I was about to encounter.

We spent the very first night of the trip in New York City. I had never seen sin and immorality like I saw in New York City. I remember going down 42nd Street, and there was a line of prostitutes lined up against the wall. I didn't know what they were doing there. I had lived such a sheltered life that it never dawned on me that women would sell their bodies. I had heard of it, but it wasn't something I thought about, so the reality of why those women were standing on the street corner didn't occur to me. I went down the road and talked to every one of those prostitutes about Jesus. I passed out Gospel tracts and told them about the love of God. The whole street emptied out. All the prostitutes left.

I was witnessing in alleyways to groups of young men at two in the morning, oblivious to the fact that they were gang members. I had a pimp try to sell me one of his girls, but he was using street language and terminology that I wasn't familiar with. I couldn't tell what he was trying to say. He talked to me for five or ten minutes, but finally threw his hands up in disgust and walked away. My friend had to explain to me that he was trying to sell me a prostitute.

My point is that I wasn't at all tempted by the things I saw. It wasn't that I had never heard of the sin that I encountered in New York City, but I'd never given it a lot of thought. I had never meditated on or turned those things over in my mind. I was focused on God. As a result, my heart was hardened toward sin, and none of it tempted me in the least.

Another way of looking at this is that you can't go anywhere in life that you haven't already been to in your mind. Imagine being in an underground tunnel: you have to excavate the rock or dirt in front of you before you can move forward. Only after you have hollowed out some space can you move on. In the same way, you can't get into sexual immorality if you haven't already thought about it. You can't get into strife, bitterness, hatred, fear, or anything else until you first of all go there in your mind.

As a man thinks in his heart, that is the way he will be (Proverbs 23:7). Change the way you think, and you will change your experience of life. As you neglect the things of this world and focus on God, your heart will become sensitive to Him and you'll begin to receive all of the benefits that go along with relationship with God such as healing, joy, peace, prosperity, and anointing.

The reason a lot of people aren't experiencing the power of God isn't because they don't believe; it's because they are neglecting the things of God, and they are too occupied with the affairs of this life.

The cares of this world, and the deceitfulness of riches, and the lusts of other things entering in, choke the word, and it becometh unfruitful.

Mark 4:19

Jesus was describing a heart condition here. When our hearts are focused on the cares of this life, the deceitfulness of riches, and the lust of other things, those distractions enter in and choke out the Word of God that has been planted in our hearts. For instance, we know that God wants to give us a life abundant with joy and peace, but many believers don't have joy or peace because the cares of life, the deceitfulness of riches, and the desire for things are taking all of their time and attention. Their hearts have become hardened, and they aren't fully receiving the benefits of God's love.

The cure for a hard heart is prayer and fasting. When the disciples failed to cast a demon out of a possessed boy, Jesus told them that their problem was unbelief. He didn't tell them they needed more faith, He told them they needed *less* unbelief (Matthew 17:20-21). A hardened heart is dominated by the mind and the senses. Prayer and fasting is a way of denying the flesh and its desires so that your focus can shift to God. Basically, it sensitizes your heart to God.

In order to experience the fullness of relationship with God, we have to change our focus. Jesus commanded us not to worry about the issues of this life because He didn't want us to get distracted from what is really important: Seeking the kingdom of God. To have a heart that is sensitive to God, you have to spend time meditating in His Word and considering the things of God. Your thoughts can't be dominated by the cares of this world and your senses. Change the way you think, harden your heart to the world, and you will begin to experience the fullness of the abundant life that God desires for you.

Additional Resources:

1.*Hardness of Heart* is a four-part audio teaching available to listen to or download for free at http://www.awmi.net/extra/audio/1003

2.*The Hardness of Heart* book by Andrew Wommack deals with the crisis, the cause, and the cure for a hardened heart. It is available through bookstores or the online store at http://www.awmi.net/store/usa/books/303

3.*Lessons from David* is a four-part audio teaching that looks at the life of David, the only person the Lord called "a man after mine own heart," and makes direct applications to our lives today. It is available to listen to or download for free at http://www.awmi.net/extra/audio/1041

How to Prepare Your Heart is a three-part audio series that will teach you what the Bible says about setting our affections and how to do it. It is available to listen to or download for free at http://www.awmi.net/extra/audio/1010

Chapter 16

Self-Centeredness: the Root of All Grief

Everyone thinks that a teaching about self-centeredness doesn't apply to them—it's always for somebody else. If you are alive and breathing, you have a "self," and I can promise you that "self" is something you have to deal with. Our culture has become very self-centered. This is not even looked down upon. In fact, it's promoted. The self-promotion that people freely engage in today would have been considered the height of arrogance a generation or two ago. Contrary to popular culture, however, self-centeredness is not a desirable quality.

We should be striving to be humble, but I'm not talking about becoming a doormat and allowing people to walk all over you. You can be a confident person with strong convictions and still be humble. Please don't think I am implying that I have totally dealt with all self-centeredness in my life, because you can't ever be delivered of "self." The only way to be delivered of self is to die. Until then, you are going to struggle against being self-centered, because it is the nature of self to want to satisfy its desires.

The problem with putting yourself first is that you end up hurting other people by ignoring their needs. Jesus is our example for living a holy life, and He was the most selfless person who ever

153

walked on this earth. Jesus didn't become a man because He needed anything. Jesus became a man because we needed something, and He gave His life to save us. Even as He was on the cross in terrible suffering, He said, "Father, forgive them; for they know not what they do" (Luke 23:34). We need to follow Jesus' example of humility.

We should be esteeming others as better than ourselves (Philippians 2:3), but there aren't many people who would even view that as a goal—much less pursue it. Yet Scripture teaches that we are supposed to love other people, and turn the other cheek to reproach (Matthew 5:39). We are intended to *endure* things for the sake of other people, which implies doing something our flesh doesn't want to.

Whether you realize it or not, your self-centeredness is the root of all of your grief. The book of Proverbs says,

> *Only by pride cometh contention: but with the well advised is wisdom.*
>
> *Proverbs 13:10*

The idea that pride is the true source of discord in our lives is radically different from what most people think. It doesn't say pride is "one of" the leading causes of conflict, or that it is more common for certain personality types. It says that pride is the *only* reason for contention. There is no other source, no other reason, and no other explanation for contention other than pride. Scripture also reveals that contention is the beginning of strife:

> *The beginning of strife is as when one letteth out water: therefore leave off contention, before it be meddled with.*
>
> *Proverbs 17:14*

Self-Centeredness: the Root of All Grief

You don't just jump from having a life filled with love and harmony into strife all at once. It's a progressive process, and the first step is contention. Pride and self-centeredness lead to contention, which opens the door to strife. Most people think that they get angry because of the things that other people say and do to them. We don't think of ourselves as being the source of the strife in our lives, but we are. What other people do doesn't cause disharmony—our own self-centeredness does, and pride is the root of it all.

I had a man approach me one night after I had preached on this subject. He said that he enjoyed what I said, but he didn't agree. He told me that he had a lot of strife in his life, and he had an anger problem, but he didn't have a pride issue. He said he had the exact opposite problem: he had no self-esteem or self-confidence at all.

What he didn't understand is that arrogance is only one manifestation of pride. Exalting yourself is one way that pride shows itself, but timidity and low self-esteem are also signs of pride rearing its ugly head. They are opposite behaviors, but the source of both is the same. Just like a stick has two ends, arrogance and timidity are opposite ends of the same issue. Pride, at its root, is just self-centeredness, and whether you are conceited or cower from attention, the root cause is pride. It doesn't matter whether you think you are better than everybody else, or if you think you are a nobody, both attitudes are self-centered.

Moses is a striking example of biblical humility. He wrote, "Now the man Moses was very meek, above all the men which were upon the face of the earth" (Numbers 12:3). Moses led three million Jews out of Egypt so there must have been several million

155

people on earth at the time, and Moses was the meekest of them all. What is even more striking is that Moses wrote this statement about himself. We have been taught a religious concept of humility that says we should knock ourselves down and have a low sense of self worth, but that isn't humility. By that way of thinking, Moses couldn't have written that he was the meekest man on earth and still have been meek.

Meekness doesn't mean you never have anything positive to say about yourself. True humility means not clinging to an opinion of yourself one way or the other. You don't exalt yourself above what you should, nor do you debase yourself. Humility is simply acknowledging what is true.

The religious idea of humility is that you play coy and never admit how good you *really* think you are. It's an attitude that is actually tangled up with pride. I think of it like a person who stands up before their congregation and says, "You know, I don't have a very good voice but God said make a joyful noise, so everyone just pray for me as I try to sing today." Then the person starts singing and she has an incredible voice. Later on you find out she had ten years of operatic training. Religion would approve of the way she downplayed her talents and abilities, but this is not an example of humility. Downplaying our abilities like that is an attempt to set a low expectation that we know we can blow out of the water. That way when we're done, everyone will be extra impressed with how great we were. It's an attempt to fish for compliments, or an effort to conform to the religious idea of humility that is being promoted today.

Try going up to someone like the woman in my example and saying, "You know, you were right: you can't sing," and then agree with all of the negative things the person said about herself. You'll find out real quickly that she didn't really believe what she was saying. We have just been taught that humility means debasing ourselves.

True humility means you don't have an agenda of self-promotion. You don't exalt yourself and you don't debase yourself, because you aren't focused on "self" at all. A humble person isn't concerned about the opinions of other people. God inspired Moses to write that he was the meekest person on the planet and he did it, because he wasn't self-focused. Not being self-centered, he could express the truth without falling into the trap of exalting himself.

Imagine you are sitting in a room full of one hundred people and someone says, "Let's all pray and ask God to reveal who is the meekest person in the room. If God tells you that you are the meekest, then stand up and let us know." Somebody in the room has to be the meekest person. If the Lord told you that you were that person, would you be humble enough to stand up and identify yourself? If considering that possibility causes you to wonder what other people would think about you when you stood up, then you're thinking about yourself. That's self-centered. A humble person isn't self-centered.

Pride, at its core, is just self-centeredness. As a whole, the Church has only criticized arrogance as pride, but low self-esteem and debasing oneself are also forms of pride. They are both examples of self-centeredness and being worried about other people's opinions.

I can say this with great conviction because I was an extreme introvert when I was a teenager. I couldn't even look a person in the face and talk to them. I was painfully shy. Some people might say, "Well, that was just your personality type." No, it was self-centeredness. Shyness, or timidity, is extreme self-centeredness—it's just a different manifestation of pride than arrogance is. I can tell you what I was thinking that caused me to be timid: I was always thinking about me, and what other people thought about me. I was so afraid of other people's criticism that I wouldn't open up and talk to people. I was afraid I might say something that would make me sound dumb.

I have met a lot of people whom God has miraculously delivered from terrible things. God has healed their marriage, delivered them from sickness, or provided finances, but they don't want to get up in front of a group of people and talk about it because they are too shy. They don't want to stand up and give their testimony because they are worried about what other people think. They have a revelation of God in an area that could change people's lives, but their focus on self stops them from helping others. Fear of other people's opinions and fear of embarrassment are just self-centeredness. It's one of the tools that Satan uses to hold people in bondage. You can describe pride with a lot of different terms, but the bottom line is that it is self-centeredness.

The things people say and do to us aren't what cause us to be angry and bitter; it's our pride and self-focus that make us react that way. Jesus said,

Self-Centeredness: the Root of All Grief

Whosoever will come after me, let him deny himself, and take up his cross, and follow me.

Mark 8:34

A cross is something you die on. To "take up" our cross means that we are supposed to die to ourselves and follow Jesus. The reason it hurts so much when people insult or criticize us is because we aren't dead to ourselves. We brood over insults and fan the flames until we see the perpetrator as having inflicted a huge injustice upon us. No one enjoys suffering wrong, but it's really our own pride that causes us to feel so hurt. If you are dead to yourself, people can insult you all they want and it won't bother you one bit. You can go down to the morgue, pull out a corpse and spit on, insult, or assault it all you want—it isn't going to respond. Dead people don't take offense.

Jesus showed us a model of putting others before ourselves. While He was on the cross, Jesus asked the Father to forgive those who crucified Him (Luke 23:34). He was more concerned for them than He was focused on His own situation. This attitude is outside of the norm, but the Bible says that the works Jesus did we should do also (John 14:12). We should be imitating Jesus' self*less*ness instead of embracing a culture of self-centeredness.

Total selflessness is a level of perfection that isn't achievable in this life, but we can start heading in that direction. I haven't arrived at selflessness, but I've left.

Back when I was pastoring a small church in Colorado, I had an elder in my church who was spreading horrible rumors about me. He said I was a liar, that I was stealing money from the church, doing drugs, and that I was committing adultery. I did confront him about the things he was saying, but his lies didn't offend me much. I knew none of it was true, and I really loved the guy, so mostly I just prayed for him.

About a week after I prayed for him, I was driving by his business with my wife. I pulled into the parking lot and asked her if she wanted to come in with me and visit with him. "No!" she said, "I don't want to go see him." So I went in alone and talked with him for a while, but he was very cold toward me. When I came back out, I said to Jamie, "Something is wrong. He wasn't friendly to me at all." Jamie looked at me funny for a moment and then she asked, "Don't you remember what happened last week?"

I had completely forgotten. Jamie had to remind me that this man had been spreading lies about me all over town in an effort to run me out of the church. It was because I loved him and was concerned for him that I had forgotten the things he said. Love will cause us to act differently from the world.

> *Love endures long and is patient and kind; love never is envious nor boils over with jealousy, is not boastful or vainglorious, does not display itself haughtily.*
>
> *It is not conceited (arrogant and inflated with pride); it is not rude (unmannerly) and does not act unbecomingly. Love (God's love in us) does not insist on its own rights or its own way, for it is not self-seeking; it is not touchy or fretful or resentful; it takes no account of the evil done to it [it pays no attention to a suffered wrong].*
>
> *1 Corinthians 13:4-5, Amplified Bible*

Self-Centeredness: the Root of All Grief

God's kind of love doesn't even notice a wrong suffered. When you are thinking more about the other person than you are about yourself, you won't be hurt. You won't take things to heart the way most people do. Our culture today is so far removed from godly principles that we don't even realize how far off base we are in what many of us consider normal behavior. Most people are selfish to the max, and will stab anybody in the back to get what they want. That might be normal in our culture, but it isn't the way God wants us to act.

When you start loving other people more and focusing on their needs, you die to yourself. You stop getting mad every time someone insults you. Getting rid of self-centeredness is just like defusing a bomb: you won't explode into anger anymore. You can still hate sin and the damage it does to people, but you won't take the same offense when somebody wrongs you. Anger is simply another manifestation of pride. It isn't in your genes, and it isn't the way you were made. It's a result of being self-centered.

Aside from getting angry at others, pride also brings up the issue of placing blame. Adam started it all in the Garden. When God asked Adam what had happened after he and Eve ate the fruit from the tree of the knowledge of good and evil, Adam said, "Lord, it's that woman that *You* gave me" (Genesis 3:12). He pointed the finger at Eve, and then tried to blame God for it! Far too many people have never accepted responsibility for anything. They are never at fault. It's always everyone else who is to blame.

It is a part of our sin nature that we are born into this world self-centered. A baby is the most selfish creature on the planet. When a baby is hungry, it cries and screams until it is fed. When you were a baby, you didn't care how much your fit throwing disrupted the world around you, because you were only thinking about yourself. The problem is that some of us have never gone beyond that selfishness. If you haven't, you could be a thirty-, forty-, or fifty-year-old adult brat, still crying and screaming to get your way. You have probably developed more sophisticated methods than temper tantrums, but if you're self-centered, you're still pitching fits.

As followers of Jesus, it's time for us to grow up. We can't control how other people treat us, but we can control ourselves. Self-centeredness is the source of grief in our lives, and the Word of God says that if you want to be free from strife and bitterness, you need to die to yourself and follow Jesus. Put your focus on God and love God more than you love yourself. Once you love God and receive His love for you, the selfless love that Jesus expressed will flow through you toward other people. You'll see a difference in your attitude. Seek God first and love other people more than yourself. As you do, the hurt and pain in your life will begin to evaporate.

Self-Centeredness: the Root of All Grief

Additional Resources:

1.*Self-Centeredness: The Root of All Grief* is an audio teaching available to listen to or download for free at http://www.awmi.net/extra/audio/sk07

2.*Self-Centeredness: The Source of All Grief* is a booklet by Andrew Wommack that discusses how difficult situations have a way of revealing the heart, and how love, joy, and peace can be yours—even in the worst of situations. It is available through the online store at http://www.awmi.net/store/usa/books/315

3.*The Christian Survival Kit* is a sixteen-part audio teaching that details how Jesus' instructions to His disciples the night before His crucifixion told them what they needed to know to keep them from being overcome with grief during this trying time. It is available to listen to or download for free at http://www.awmi.net/extra/audio/1001

4.*Lessons from Elijah* is a five-part audio teaching that covers the scriptural example that Elijah provides—both good and bad. It is available to listen to or download for free at http://www.awmi.net/extra/audio/1026

5.*How to Deal with Grief* is a four-part audio teaching. Grief is something that each one of us encounters sooner or later. It cannot be avoided, but it can be dealt with in a positive way. This teaching will show you how; it is available to listen to or download for free at http://www.awmi.net/extra/audio/1032

God's Kind of Love to You is a five-part audio teaching that shows how our heavenly Father is a God of Love. It is available to listen to or download for free at http://www.awmi.net/extra/audio/1054

About the Author

For over three decades, Andrew Wommack has traveled America and the world teaching the truth of the Gospel. His profound revelation of the Word of God is taught with clarity and simplicity, emphasizing God's unconditional love and the balance between grace and faith.

He reaches millions of people through the daily "Gospel Truth" radio and television programs, broadcast both domestically and internationally. He founded Charis Bible College in 1994 and has since established CBC extension schools in other major cities of America and around the world.

Andrew has produced a library of teaching materials—available in print, audio, and visual formats. And, as it has been from the beginning, his ministry continues to distribute free audio tapes and CDs to those who cannot afford them.

To contact Andrew Wommack please write, e-mail, or call:

Andrew Wommack Ministries
P.O. Box 3333 • Colorado Springs, CO 80934-3333
E-mail: awommack@aol.com
Helpline Phone (orders and prayer): 719-635-1111
Hours: 4:00 AM to 9:30 PM MST

Andrew Wommack Ministries of Europe
P.O. Box 4392 • WS1 9AR Walsall • England
E-mail: enquiries@awme.net

U.K. Helpline Phone (orders and prayer):
011-44-192-247-3300
Hours: 5:30 AM to 4:00 PM GMT

Or visit him on the Web at: **www.awmi.net**

Receive Jesus as Your Savior

Choosing to receive Jesus Christ as your Lord and Savior is the most important decision you'll ever make!

God's Word promises, *"That if thou shalt confess with thy mouth the Lord Jesus, and shalt believe in thine heart that God hath raised him from the dead, thou shalt be saved. For with the heart man believeth unto righteousness; and with the mouth confession is made unto salvation"* (Romans 10:9-10). *"For whosoever shall call upon the name of the Lord shall be saved"* (Romans 10:13).

By His grace, God has already done everything to provide salvation. Your part is simply to believe and receive.

Pray out loud, *"Jesus, I confess that You are my Lord and Savior. I believe in my heart that God raised You from the dead. By faith in Your Word, I receive salvation now. Thank You for saving me!"*

The very moment you commit your life to Jesus Christ, the truth of His Word instantly comes to pass in your spirit. Now that you're born again, there's a brand-new you!

Please contact me and let me know that you've prayed to receive Jesus as your Savior or to be filled with the Holy Spirit. I would like to rejoice with you and help you understand more fully what has taken place in your life. I'll send you a free gift that will help you understand and grow in your new relationship with the Lord.

Welcome to your new life!

Receive the Holy Spirit

As His child, your loving heavenly Father wants to give you the supernatural power you need to live this new life.

"For every one that asketh receiveth; and he that seeketh f indeth; and to him that knocketh it shall be opened...how much more shall your heavenly Father give the Holy Spirit to them that ask him?" (Luke11:10-13).

All you have to do is ask, believe, and receive!

Pray, *"Father, I recognize my need for Your power to live this new life. Please fill me with Your Holy Spirit. By faith, I receive it right now! Thank You for baptizing me. Holy Spirit, You are welcome in my life!"*

Congratulations—now you're filled with God's supernatural power!

Some syllables from a language you don't recognize will rise up from your heart to your mouth (1 Corinthians 14:14). As you speak them out loud by faith, you're releasing God's power from within and building yourself up in your spirit (1 Corinthians 14:4).

You can do this whenever and wherever you like.

It doesn't really matter whether you felt anything or not when you prayed to receive the Lord and His Spirit. If you believed in your heart that you received, then God's Word promises that you did. *"Therefore I say unto you, What things soever ye desire, when ye pray, believe that ye receive them, and ye shall have them"* (Mark 11:24).

God always honors His Word—believe it! Please contact me and let me know that you've prayed to receive Jesus as your Savior or to be filled with the Holy Spirit. I would like to rejoice with you and help you understand more fully what has taken place in your life. I'll send you a free gift that will help you understand and grow in your new relationship with the Lord. *Welcome to your new life!*

The Harrison House Vision

Proclaiming the truth and the power

Of the Gospel of Jesus Christ

With excellence;

Challenging Christians to

Live victoriously,

Grow spiritually,

Know God intimately.